D0225757

Neighbors — Mexico and the United States

Wetbacks and Oil

Robert Jones Shafer and Donald Mabry

Neighbors — Mexico

and the United States
Wetbacks and Oil

Nelson-Hall nh Chicago

The paper in this book is pH neutral (acid-free).

LIBRARY OF CONGRESS CATALOGING IN PUBLICATION DATA

Shafer, Robert Jones.
    Neighbors—Mexico and the United States.

    Bibliography: p.
    Includes index.
    1. United States—Foreign relations–Mexico.
2. Mexico—Foreign relations—United States.
3. Mexican Americans.   I.   Mabry, Donald J.,
1941–   .   II.   Title.
E183.8.M6S3   327.72073   81–11074
ISBN 0–88229–726–0 (cloth)   AACR2
ISBN 0–88229–781–3 (paper)

Manufactured in the United States of America

10   9   8   7   6   5   4   3   2   1

For the neighbors—
We love them both

Contents

Preface

Mexico stands out from most of the Third World nations for its size, population, social-political stability, and rapid economic growth. It stands out, also, because recent oil discoveries have turned it into a net exporter, a rare and dramatic event in this time of energy crisis. The United States especially hopes to benefit from the petroleum surpluses of its neighbor. But a host of historic and current problems complicates relations between the two countries, not the least being large immigration (often illegal, often winked at) from Mexico to the United States. Other important ingredients in relations are that Mexico is highly nationalistic and its leaders sensitive to charges of truckling to Washington and those leaders are highly trained in diplomatic, financial, and technical matters, and able to estimate to the penny (or centavo) the worth of Mexican resources. In dealing with the two countries this book is intended to illuminate the entire range of relations between them, but especially the petroleum and immigration problems. Although the authors are professional Latin Americanists, the book is meant for a broad audience. Such a book rests on a multitude of published and documentary sources, personal experiences and conversation, travels, and observations, research, teaching, speech-making in the United States and Mexico, and service in the United States government. May they serve to improve relations between the neighbors. We are citizens of one, but we love them both.

ONE

Neighbors

"A well-fed neighbor sleeps, and so may you" is a folk saying that Mexican emissaries have long quoted in Washington. Americans agreed it is a charming aphorism, yet we have declined to bear the cost of such a panacea. With wetbacks flooding the United States, we are aware, of course, that a hungry Mexico is expensive, too. But, cheap labor is useful, and the ultimate decision, it has been thought, lies with Washington, not with a weak Mexico in which the United States had little interest.

That was the thinking before the 1970s, when the OPEC oil cartel unbalanced world prices and Mexico entered its second great oil boom. To North Americans, that boom seemed a blessed way out of the OPEC trap.

Foreign relations are among the most difficult of human enterprises to manage, partly because of well-justified suspicions and fears. These often are exaggerated between next-door nations, who, like next-door neighbors, must be sensitive to each other's problems, because so many opportunities for friction arise. Cheek-by-jowl quarrels offer chances to wound that are absent from long-distance squabbling. When England

1

held much of France in medieval times, the countries constantly slashed at each other. Russia's neighbors for centuries have likened their position to that of "being in bed with an elephant," and Mexico has felt like that toward the U.S. since it became independent of Spain in 1821. Its relations with Washington often have been strained or broken, usually because they were neighbors.

Neighbors are bound to have problems along their border. There are customs laws and searches and aggravating rules and waits. There is illegal "hot pursuit" over the border of antelope, cattle, bandits, smugglers, wives, and lovers. There is the exchange of cleverer refugees—embezzlers, stock manipulators, and political terrorists—and the documentation of extradiction and legal proceedings. Goods move back and forth, legally and illegally. There is exchange of whores, strong drink and drugs, gambling, weapons, factories, blue jeans, and shoes. But now, happily, there is not much exchange of gunfire, unlike some borders in the world.

A common border increases the potential for trouble when one nation is rich and the other poor; nowhere is there a border contrast greater than that between the United States and Mexico. Such disparity promotes smuggling, illegal entry, labor abuses, arrogance, and resentment. Americans sneer that "when Mexico enters the twentieth century, real communication will be possible." Mexicans sigh, "poor Mexico, so far from God, and so near the United States."

Being next to the United States often has been a curse to Mexico, but it is now at least a mixed blessing to the swarming poor south of the border. The 65 million Mexicans of today will be more than 100 million in twenty years, while the economy, though growing, scarcely dents the legions of the poor.

So they go to the United States—on contract, under the fence, or packed into the trunks of cars. Mexican maids pour in from Ciudad Juárez daily to work in the homes of El Paso, Texas; other Mexicans cross in a thousand places to pick melons, wash cars, and swab out restaurants. Meanwhile, U.S. industry, encouraged by Mexican law, moves south of the border to use the cheap hands there.

American organized labor demands reduced contract labor from Mexico, expulsion of illegal immigrants, a curb on border factories in Mexico, and a tightly policed frontier. On the other hand, growers of lettuce and almonds say that Americans will not do "stoop" labor and that Mexican pickers are needed. Leaders in Mexico say that their poor citizens are invited to the United States and then mistreated. They also declare that Mexicans who have for years lived and worked illegally in the United States have, in effect, earned a "promise" that they may remain. Mexican newspapers claim that the United States cannot now change the "rules" and deport illegal Mexican aliens.

Mexican leaders and newspapers say, in addition, that since their country cannot provide jobs for the mushrooming population, Mexicans inevitably will cross the border illegally until the United States helps improve the Mexican economy so that Mexicans will want to stay home.

The United States says, "Have fewer babies"; Mexico says, "Mind your own business." Washington declares, "Work harder"; Mexico City replies, "Charge less for your manufactured goods and reduce tariffs on our goods." The U.S. cries, "Stop the drug traffic!" Mexico suggests, "Stop using drugs."

Mexicans also angrily complain that millions of people of Mexican heritage who are citizens of the United States meet prejudice and discrimination. The United States scarcely can answer that.

So there is friction, even when the will to compromise exists; when it does not, we hear demands for extreme "solutions"—thickets of guns, electric fences, guard dogs, a wall from sea to sea.

The friction abruptly lost much of its importance with news of vast new Mexican oil discoveries during the 1970s. North

American interest in Mexico soared. It was hoped that gas from Tabasco and oil from Vera Cruz would let Americans forget the Arabs. Washington serenaded Mexico City. Alas, the serenade was unpracticed and sung but clumsily. Could the U.S. learn to do better? Could the neighbors forge a better relationship? *Ojalá,* God willing, as the Mexicans say.

TWO

A Bad Scenario

In the crystal balls of the intelligence agencies the following unhappy future *may be* flickering.

Just after midnight, June 8, the United States closed its border with Mexico, following three years of intense national debate. Ten thousand new searchlights went on, draining power from the grids serving centers from San Diego to Brownsville, Texas. More than 200,000 treasury, immigration, police, and military personnel were in place from the Gulf of Mexico to the Pacific, an average of one hundred guards for each of the two thousand miles of the border. On roads paralleling the border—some of them newly bulldozed dirt tracks—cruise police and sheriff's cars and motorcycles, and military jeeps and armored vehicles. From new helicopter parks, choppers covered assigned sectors.

Roads and rail lines crossing the border were blocked. Air crossings were prohibited, and radar and military aircraft were in place to enforce the ban. Washington said the barriers were up until a new agreement was reached with Mexico on search procedures. Mexico said there would be no accord during the rupture of traffic by the United States.

America began a mammoth wall project, starting at the shores of the Gulf of Mexico and the Pacific Ocean and proceeding in both directions from twelve other points: Brownsville, McAllen, Laredo, Eagle Pass, Del Rio, and El Paso, in Texas; Columbus in New Mexico; Douglas, Nogales, Lukeville, and near Yuma, in Arizona; and Calexico in California. Thus, what the Mexicans at once call La Muralla del Buen Vecino—the Good Neighbor Wall—had twenty-six moving faces. The foundation went six feet below the ground, while bald, brutal concrete was to rise twenty-five feet above the surface. On top of the monstrosity were to be six feet of wire charged with lethal voltage. It was planned to clear and level the ground on both sides of the wall in strips one hundred fifty feet wide, but the details were incomplete because of protests from property owners in the border cities. Only fifty-six gates were planned in the wall. There would be a guard tower fifty feet high at one-mile intervals. The Good Neighbor Wall was one of the largest construction projects in history; for much of the world, it was one of the most obnoxious.*

Crowds gathered on both sides of the border, especially near the wall construction sites. Before noon on the first day of construction enough incidents occurred to confirm the predictions of pessimists—bombs, dynamite, bottles of gasoline, fire, rocks, clubs, guns, and knives wrecked hundreds of buildings and killed 112 and injured 1,515 persons. Most of the casualties were in the United States, but some of them were Mexican citizens as well.

Reporters, cameramen, TV technicians and makeup people, cartoonists, editorial pundits, and feature writers had flooded the border areas of the United States and Mexico. An effort to keep media personnel outside wide "security zones" on the American side soon collapsed. The zones were too extensive to police. The reporters were too insistent. Too many bystanders also were invading the zones. Neither civil nor

---

*See chapter 6 for wall and fence schemes in the 1970s.

military officials were anxious to prick TV personalities with bayonets. Yet in the end, the media contributed five dead and thirty-six injured, including nationals from eight countries. And when media people were killed and wounded, their employers and followers demanded that the United States arrange its affairs more sensibly.

"Let's be sensible, Mr. President," the majority leader of the Senate said just after noon in the White House Oval Office.

"That always is my aim, senator," the president said frostily.

The senator shrugged. "I might have phrased that better, Mr. President. I meant to say, what are we looking for, of course, is a practical solution to this immigration mess."

The president said sourly, "You know that's what Mexico's president, López Portillo, told us when he visited here in 1977, that we needed a more "sensible," policy in the Western Hemisphere. Irritating word. Anyway, closing the border and building the wall was supposed to bring Mexico into line on both immigration and petroleum policy. You supported it, senator."

The senator nodded, not apologetically: "I did. Lots of folks were for it. I'm not sure who's for it now. Maybe we made a mistake."

The president said, rather contemptuously, "Possibly. But if you change a policy during the first day's outcry against it. . . ." He did not finish the sentence.

The senator said firmly, "I just wanted you to understand that I was ready for compromise if that is necessary."

"Yes, Jim. I know you're up for reelection this fall."

The senator had been a power in national politics for twenty years and knew better than to accept such a sneer without retaliation. "I'll tell you, Walt," he told the president, "that sort of tone gets a lot of people's backs up."

The president smiled with effort and said, "I know. I shouldn't have said it, Jim."

At 4:00 P.M., the National Security Council heard a lot about people whose backs were up.

The secretary of state summarized world reaction to the wall. "Communists claim brutality, imperialism, lack of respect for developing nations. So does the noncommunist Third World. The Organization of African States is preparing a statement. The Human Rights Commission of the Organization of American States is in session at the request of Mexico. Four organs of the United Nations have issued or are preparing condemnations of our policy."

The president complained. "All those countries control entry by foreigners. The Soviets built quite a wall in Germany."

"Yes," the secretary said. "We have a statement going out today that includes those points."

"The strong reaction surprised you, too?"

"Yes, Mr. President. The name the Mexicans gave the wall helped dramatize it, and so did the size of the wall."

The president said impatiently, "I know you were against it. So it's too bad we didn't knock off a few feet." He looked at another figure seated at the long table. "Organized labor had no doubts."

The labor secretary was famed for his bluntness. Up from the ranks, he strove for (and overdid) the common touch. "Mr. President," he said, "I've talked to nearly fifty labor leaders, and they say we sure have a right to protect ourselves against cheap foreign labor. They say the issue of closing the border was fully debated, absolutely fully and democratically debated. And they say, also, Mr. President, that Mexico controls its own immigration with an iron fist, but says we can't. They say, "Let's show 'em.' They say we hope our security forces will learn how to control terrorist elements in the border area."

"We all hope that," the president dryly agreed, looking at the secretary of defense.

The secretary of defense had great technical ability and a short way with those he thought his intellectual inferiors. "We know how to do it now, Mr. President, but the guidelines laid down have made it difficult. You can't control mobs, or journalists, with scolding."

"We all agree with that, too," the president said sharply. "And we all know that Mexico is bound to retaliate through its petroleum policy."

He looked at the secretary of state, who shrugged and said, "I don't see that anything has changed. We either give in to pressure or not."

The president said grimly, "We'll give the security forces more authority." He looked around the table and asked harshly, "Is there any dissent?"

So, that night a butter-toned TV newsperson reported, "The administration position is that it's a sensible, legitimate, and necessary policy that must be supported more firmly. Critics say that it means a dictatorship—at least in the border area."

But most Americans did not believe that a dictatorship was in the making. Mostly, they were irritated. They thought that immigration was something each nation should control for itself. Could anyone enter the Soviet Union, take a job from a Russian, get welfare and public medical care? No, and anyone couldn't go to Mexico and do that either. But Mexicans could do it in the United States. And they could riot against American law, as many people, to their irritation, saw on television.

What the media publicized as the first violence was the killing of Patricio Guardiola Ramírez, twenty, a third-year student at the University of Nuevo León in the city of Monterrey, one hundred twenty miles south of the border city of Laredo, Texas. All his life, Patricio, from a middle-class business family, had heard praise or envy of United States' economic achievements and condemnation of its Mexican policies. When, three years before, Washington hardened its views on immigration, Patricio was prepared to be indignant. Student attitudes were at least formally leftist and they were passionately nationalist. Nearly all students disliked gringo investments and branch plants in Mexico and gringo barriers to imports of Mexico's tomatoes, shoes, and other products.

Patricio and forty-three other students drove to Nuevo Laredo, in the state of Tamaulipas, then waded the shallow Rio Grande (called the Rio Bravo in Mexico) three miles east of the center of Laredo, Texas. From there they walked back to where construction had begun on the wall just outside the city. It was one hundred fifty feet from the river, leaving a cleared zone to expose saboteurs coming from Mexico. The lights illuminated a strip more than a quarter-mile square, crowded with earth-moving vehicles, piles of lumber and steel for concrete forms, other building equipment and materials, soldiers and police and their vehicles, media personnel, with television cables snaking in all directions, and several thousand spectators interested enough to stand in a field at 12:43 A.M.

The forty-four students from the University of Nuevo León appproached a group of eight or ten U.S. soldiers, who were standing near some big concrete mixing trucks whose fat bodies revolved, leaking a grey-white liquid. The students yelled, "Viva México!" and threw some rocks at the soldiers. Patricio Guardiola Ramírez may have thrown the first stone, but he did not hit anyone. Some other stones broke off four of the teeth of a U.S. Army private named Edgar Prentice Brownlaw, from Cleveland Heights, Ohio. In his rage and pain and fear he shot Patricio Guardiola Ramírez dead. Since Patricio was shot in the head, the television cameras got a perfectly dreadful picture of the young man's face disintegrating.

The army officers commanding the area efficiently buttoned things up. The forty-three surviving students were escorted to the international bridge. A funeral home in Laredo carried the body of Patricio Guardiola Ramírez to a funeral home in Nuevo Laredo. Private Brownlaw was hustled out of the area and never was interviewed or punished.

The news came to the million residents of the twin cities of Ciudad Juárez in the state of Chihuahua, and El Paso, Texas. Over two-thirds of those people live in Mexico, and many of them cross daily over a bridge to work and shop in El Paso. Smaller numbers of Americans go to Ciudad Juárez to buy handcrafted furniture, rugs, jewelry, wrought iron, glass, and ceramics. Servicemen from the big American air and army bases nearby also go to the bars, nightclubs, and whorehouses of Juárez.

Mexicans who went to the bridge in the early morning of June 8 found the gates closed and guarded by soldiers. A big sign said

ESTA CLAUSURADO EL PUENTE—BRIDGE CLOSED.

A crowd built up at the Mexican end of the bridge. It was noisy but orderly, mostly made up of ordinary citizens who wanted to go to El Paso, as they did every day. A handful of nationalists and agitators shouted slogans, but few people paid attention. That was going to change.

It was going to change because in El Paso a man named Harry Crane thought the death of Patricio Guardiola Ramírez presented him with an opportunity. There were 3,472 other U.S. citizens who thought that the Mexican sutdent's death must offer an oppportunity, but few of them could decide what the opportunity was. Crane was in no doubt: It was an excuse for violence that would bring American institutions into disrepute, for Crane belonged to a tiny group, The Clarifiers, that rages against the impurity of human society.

Crane and his colleagues paid a Mexican who was illegally in El Paso to go back across the border into Ciudad Juárez with Crane. The Mexican carried a portable loudspeaker in a suitcase, while Crane had two Molotov cocktails in a paper shopping bag marked in big letters

OAK STREET SHOPPING CENTER, AIR CONDITIONED.

There were about 10,000 people now at the Mexican end of the international bridge, mostly quiet, smoking, buying tacos, roasted corn, and flavored waters from vendors. The

Mexican army lieutenant in command of the squad of fifteen soldiers behind the flimsy gates at the entrance to the bridge was relaxed. He knew that the police and army had rounded up every known troublemaker in the Ciudad Juárez area. He knew the crowd would go home as soon as it was convinced that it could not get across the river.

Harry Crane and his hired hand made their way to the front of the crowd at the gate. At 9:32 A.M. that morning of June 8, the hired hand took the portable loudspeaker out of his suitcase and began screaming:

A LA MURALLA! A LA MURALLA! A LA MURALLA!
TO THE WALL! TO THE WALL! TO THE WALL!

That was a cry that not only referred to the new Good Neighbor Wall but to all walls against which so many men had been executed throughout history. It had been a popular slogan during Castro's revolution in Cuba.

The crowd surged forward against the gate at the entrance to the bridge. The army lieutenant talked rapidly into a telephone. As the gates bulged under the crowd's pressure, the lieutenant slammed down the phone and ordered his men to the sides of the bridge. The shouting crowd pushed down the gate and flowed across the bridge toward the heavy barricade at the American end, where a loudspeaker bellowed:

ALTO AHI! DETENGANSE! SI NO, DISPARAMOS!
STOP THERE! HALT! IF NOT, WE WILL SHOOT!

Harry Crane ran out ahead of the crowd, which began to slow its advance. He gripped a Molotov cocktail with a burning fuse. Behind him, reluctantly and far behind, came his hired hand with the shopping bag containing the other gasoline bomb. Crane ran close to the barricade at the United States end of the bridge and threw the bottle of gasoline. It burst in a sheet of flame between two soldiers, and their screams could be heard for a quarter of a mile.

A U.S. Army captain shouted FIRE! and a burst of carbine and machine pistol fire continued for nearly fifteen seconds, until a lieutenant colonel got his CEASE FIRE! heard and obeyed.

By then, as a later count showed, 32 Mexicans were dead on the bridge and 117 wounded. The Mexican dead included the man carrying the shopping bag. Also dead was Harry Crane.

By 10:30 A.M. the president of the United States knew that the fingerprints of the man who threw the bomb were those of Harry G. Crane, member of the anarchistic Clarifiers. The Mexican ambassador was informed. He phoned Mexico City.

At noon the president of Mexico released the text of a protest his ambassador to Washington was to was to deliver simultaneously to the president of the United States:

The government of Mexico protests in the strongest terms:

1. The interruption of traffic between its territory and that of the United States of North America by a unilateral action of the government of the latter.

2. The construction of a wall of such exaggerated characteristics as to suggest that the attitude of the United States toward the United Mexican States is one of profound mistrust and lack of cordiality.

3. The killing early today by United States troops of Patricio Guardiola Ramírez, a Mexican citizen and a student guilty of nothing more reprehensible than throwing a rock.

4. The slaughter of Mexican citizens on the international bridge between Ciudad Juárez and El Paso by United States military action far in excess of what was required to handle disturbed conditions there, conditions aggravated by the criminal activities of a United States citizen.

At 12:15 P.M. the United States ambassador in Mexico was informed that the Mexican Congress insisted on revising the terms under which United States capital—possibly $3 billion worth—operated in Mexico.

At 12:30 the Mexican government announced that all United States citizens residing in Mexico—twenty thousand or so—were required to apply for new identity cards and supply new information about their economic affairs and their ties with institutions in the United States, especially the federal government and its intelligence agencies.

At 12:38, at the medical faculty buildings of the University of Guadalajara, riots began against U.S. students there—some twelve hundred of them. Nearly eighty were injured; most suffered property damage. Mexican troops put all American students under protective custody in a warehouse. Some 90 percent of the students left Mexico in the next few days.

At 1:00 P.M. the Mexican government announced agreement with the USSR and Cuba for negotiation of new economic ties to emphasize minerals, industrial goods, and petroleum products. Moscow hinted that the Soviet oil on which Cuba depended might be replaced by supplies from Mexico.

That same morning of June 8 a decision was taken by another of the 3,473 United States citizens who saw the death of Patricio Guardiola Ramírez as an opportunity. Billy Joe Pope of Nogales, Arizona, decided that Ramírez's death justified assassination of the president of the United States for not being tough enough with "greasers," as Billy Joe called Mexicans, though not to their faces. Mexicans were responsible, Billy Joe knew, for his failures in school, at work, and with women. He didn't go to his job as cook in a restaurant that day because he had to plan the assassination. He did that in great and loving detail until, at 2:30 P.M., his TV set informed him that the governor of Arizona had arrived in Nogales to be sure that calm had been restored at the border. The TV screen showed the governor chatting with a crowd at a border station. Many people in the crowd obviously were of Latin or Indian extraction. Billy Joe abruptly decided that the governor was as much a Mexican-lover as the president.

He rushed down to the border station, only a few blocks

from his rented downtown room. It proved simple to walk up to the governor and shoot him twice in the stomach.

The media in the United States wallowed in fear and recrimination. Spokesmen of every interest group and point of view issued statements, often critical of the administration, though calling for national solidarity in perilous—if mismanaged—times. The president of the United States watched TV for fifteen minutes, alternately enraged at what he considered excessive Mexican pressure, and yet fearful of what was happening to his own political position.

And so attending a National Security Councity meeting at four that afternoon he found it a mess. All present were as irritated and fearful as the president. Partisans of moderation and advocates of a "policy of national strength" were equally firm—and deaf. The president finally decided in favor of a show of national strength.

Thus, appearing on national prime time TV, the president began, "Fellow Americans, I have issued orders that security on our border with Mexico be strengthened. I say to you that attacks on United States armed personnel will not be tolerated." He also asked American citizens to rally in defense of their right to set internal policy, reminding them that border and immigration policy had been decided over several years after the fullest debate.

The president hoped that recent events and his own reactions had increased rather than diminished his support, but he had no idea if that was the case. His friends assured him all was well, his foes hinted at impeachment, and network pundits pointed out that more than one ass had inhabited the White House.

The TV networks interviewed John Whipple, mayor of El Paso, at 8:00 P.M. that night.

Q: Mr. Mayor, as you have heard, there has been violence all along the border. Do you suppose the causes are the same everywhere?

A: Yes.

Q: What are those causes, Mr. Mayor?

A: A lot of impractical theorists tried to solve a complex social, economic, international problem too abruptly and without proper attention to fact and to the opinions of those who know the facts best—that is, the people who live in the border area.

Q: You do agree, I suppose, Mayor Whipple, that immigration policy is a national, not a local, problem?

A: Putting a twenty-five-foot wall through our town makes it more important to us than to Boston or Buffalo.

Q: Of course, the wall hasn't been started inside El Paso.

A: No, and I hope it won't be.

But when the president sent another 100,000 troops to the border area, including more than 8,000 to El Paso, Mayor Whipple went on the air to ask that his constituents receive the troops quietly as fellow citizens going about their duty, even if that duty included clearing a strip through El Paso.

One hundred and fifty-three professors, churchmen, artists, and writers took an ad in the *New York Times* deploring the administration's arrogance, the influence of military men outside their proper sphere, and the role played in American foreign policy by profit-motivated energy corporations.

The president of Mexico, by June 15, was short of sleep, short of temper, and short of solutions. At 11:00 P.M. he was conferring with a small group of advisers at Los Pinos, his residence in Chapultepec Park.

"I hope," he observed testily, "that no one else will inform me that world opinion is on our side. Unfortunately, the United States on its side has economic strength and military power.'" He nodded at the minister of government—an old friend and a man known for his hardheadedness and lack of interest in ideological considerations.

"The possibility," the minister said, "of cutting off the flow of petroleum and natural gas to the United States has again been considered, and decided in the negative. The president directs me to announce that there will be no further discussion of that issue."

The president nodded curtly and said, "We will again communicate to the world press, the United States, the United Nations, the Organization of American States, and other agencies our firm desire for a negotiated compromise. We will emphasize violent and unilateral United States actions and play down the possibility of further retaliation by Mexico.'" He shrugged. "We will try it for a while. The United States is very near and other powers very far."

Unable to contain his indignation, the minister of labor cried, "It's a surrender!"

"It's sensible,'" the president said flatly.

"It's statesmanlike," declared the minister of government.

"It's final,'" said the president.

At 1:33 A.M., July 19, the president of the United States was sleepy, angry, and frustrated. He looked without admiration at the seventeen advisers who had been at the long table in the White House for three hours.

"To sum up our deliberations," the president said acidly, "the Mexicans have outmaneuvered us. Or, we made a mistake and they pounced on it. Unhandsome of them." He stood up and said bluntly, "Construction of the wall will cease at once."

An opposition senator shouted, "It's a surrender!"

"Oh, for the love of Christ!" the president snarled, and stalked from the room.

The world saw excellent TV shots of the abortive Good Neighbor Wall, beginning in the surf of the Gulf of Mexico and marching starkly inland for 4.76 miles to its full height of twenty-five feet, then another 1.69 miles at only fifteen feet high, and .34 miles that only reach ten feet. Pieces like that were strung over the 2,000 miles of the border, iron reinforcing rods sticking up from the uncompleted sections, the great cranes standing idle, mountains of supplies under tied-down tarps.

"With the wall mess out of the way," said the president, "we should be able to handle the problem."

The Senate majority leader nodded. "Yes, Mr. President.

Think we should knock down the parts that were built?"

"Later, I would say, when it's lost most of its news value." The president shook his head. "Most of us thought the wall was a necessary part of the solution—if we really wanted a solution."

"Yes, I know, Walt," the senator agreed gloomily. "The reaction surprised all of us."

"You know, Jim, I still think there's a lot of support for cutting immigration, including Mexican."

"Well, sure, Mr. President. That's why we voted for the wall. It'll be tougher without it."

The president nodded emphatically, "We don't want two or three hundred thousand troops on the border all the time.'"

The senator said sarcastically, "Maybe we should take the Mexican suggestion: make Mexico rich and then people won't want to leave."

"How many votes can you round up for that, Jim?"

"Maybe not even my own."

"Then maybe there's no solution."

The senator said firmly, "Sure there is, Mr. President; it's the pricing we need to get straight."

"Yeah," the president said, without enthusiasm. "The price of oil. For the first time I'm glad it's my second term."

THREE

The Long Border

The long border is sun, sand, rocks, and mountains. It is cactus, creosote bush, yucca, and candlewood. Green strips border the Rio Grande and other streams and irrigation channels. The long border runs nearly 2,000 miles from the Gulf of Mexico following the Rio Grande northwest to El Paso. Although 1,200 miles by the river's winding course, it is only 685 straight-line miles from the Gulf. From El Paso west, the border is a surveyed line along the western half of New Mexico's southern border, then the Arizona and California lines to the Pacific just south of San Diego.

The Border Country

At the Gulf of Mexico the border is barely south of 26 degrees latitude, about level with Miami. Then it follows the mid-point of the Rio Grande northwest to 31 degrees 47 minutes at El Paso, about the latitude of Savannah, Georgia. From there it goes west 100 miles, then south to parallel 31 degrees 21 minutes, then west to longitude 111 degrees at Nogales, Arizona, where it slants northwest to the Colorado

River at a point 20 miles below its junction with the Gila River at Yuma, Arizona. From near Yuma the line runs west to the Pacific Ocean, slightly north of the latitude of El Paso.

Border elevations rise slowly from the Gulf of Mexico to 420 feet above sea level at Laredo, Texas, 180 miles from the Gulf; and 1,461 feet at Eagle Pass-Piedras Negras, 290 miles from the Gulf. After that the land rises into the mountainous Great Bend country of the Rio Grande, where the river runs through canyons 1,500 feet deep. In the Chisos Mountains in Big Bend National Park not far from the Rio Grande, Emory Peak rises to 7,800 feet. Then the river passes through the fertile El Paso-Ciudad Juárez Valley, 85 miles long and 4 miles wide. The twin cities are at an elevation of 3,800 feet in the plateau and mountain valley country of North America that stretches for thousands of miles through central Mexico and western United States.

West of El Paso the border through New Mexico and much of Arizona is generally at 3,000 to 4,000 feet. The border surveys of the 1850s noted that if the seas rose 4,000 feet, a ship could be sailed along this line, with a bit of deviation to avoid isolated peaks. At El Paso the waterway would narrow to a gunshot length from each shore, and peaks would tower above the ships.

The crow flies 270 miles from El Paso to the two Nogales, in Mexico and Arizona, where the elevation is 3,689 feet; but only 66 miles north of there, Tucson is at 2,423 feet, with a pleasant winter climate. Not far west of Nogales and continuing along the border for many miles are the Papago Indian Reservation and the Organ Pipe Cactus National Monument. Within the reservation is Kitt Peak National Observatory, on a 6,875-foot mountain only 56 miles southwest of Tucson, whose lights provide the only obstacle to astronomers in that vacant land. Near the observatory is 7,300-foot Mt. Baboquivari—the center of the universe and the home of God, according to Papago legend.

Not far west of Mt. Baboquivari, the elevation begins to fall off in the Gila River Valley. At the junction of the Gila and

Colorado rivers at Yuma—280 miles west of Nogales—the border is only 275 feet above sea level. Beyond that it is just over 200 miles from the Arizona-California line at the Colorado River to the Pacific shore.

Immediately beyond the Colorado River, the border falls into the Salton Sink, a great depression below the level of the sea, 85 miles long, 20 miles wide, and comprising the Imperial and Coachella valleys in the United States and the Mexicali Valley in Mexico. The sink once was an inland lake, and it left deep deposits of silt to make rich farmland. The line west of the sink goes over a range of mountains almost to the Pacific before dipping to the sea just south of San Diego.

South of the Salton Sink in Mexico the land falls away into the Colorado River delta for about 100 miles to the Gulf of Lower California. It is hot country, ruled much of the year by a fiery sun. Day after day it broils, often over 100 degrees. The air shimmers, mirages pop into view, and distant mountains hide in a heat haze. In the high country the fierce but dry heat of the summer day can be relieved in the cool dimness of adobe structures with thick walls; and the mountain nights are balmy. But no relief comes along the lower Colorado River and in the Great Sink of California, where temperatures reach 130° and poor farm workers sleep in the irrigation ditches.

During the brief winters cold winds bring snow to the cactus and chapparal of the high country. Even Tucson, considerably lower than El Paso or Nogales, has some frosty nights in winter. Northers come down onto the eastern half of the border country and immobilize the lizards and rattlesnakes. Storms from the Gulf sometimes come up the border through Texas and even into eastern New Mexico.

Although the whole area along the border is a sun belt, temperature varies with elevation and season, helping to define the best zones for citrus, grapes, cotton, and vegetables. Equally defining is the sparse rainfall of a thirsty country. Lakes and streams are rare. Water conservation is the first law of living organisms in the great border country. Animals lay up by day. Plants store water in their tissues, and desert animals and old prospectors know how to extract it. Dry stream gulches, subject to rare infusions of storm water, are much more common than running water.

Most of southern California gets less than ten inches of rain a year. Yuma, Arizona, enjoys less than four inches! Tucson has eleven inches and is so dry a locality that many winters pass without snow, although occasional temperatures would allow it. Spaniards drove mule trains and wagons through the Rio Grande's parched bed. Texans say it is a river that can be plowed. Even in the delta area near the Gulf of Mexico the moderate annual rainfall of about twenty-four inches falls mostly in summer, so that irrigation is needed at other times.

The great rivers are the Rio Grande and the Colorado. The Rio Grande flows 1,800 miles from the high Rockies in southern Colorado to the Gulf of Mexico, and for about the lower half of its course forms the international border. Normally shallow, sluggish, and even dry some summers, it is, nevertheless, the lifeblood of New Mexico, south Texas, and the northern parts of the Mexican states of Chihuahua, Coahuila, Nuevo León, and Tamaulipas. Although the river turns into a half-mile torrent in spring thaws or sudden storms, such occasions normally occur only between May and September. The river delivers an annual volume of some 9.38 million acre-feet, little compared with the more than 100 million spewed forth by the mighty Mississippi. The Rio Grande drains a great area of 185,000 square miles, of which 105,000 are in the United States. From its source to Ft. Quitman, south of El Paso, all the water in the river rises in the United States. The greatest tributary is the Pecos, born in the southern Sangre de Cristo Range in New Mexico and joining the Rio Grande in Texas. Below Ft. Quitman more water comes from Mexican than from United States streams; and in the end about half the water comes from each country, so in every way the Rio Grande (or Bravo) belongs to both.

The Colorado River rises in the Rocky Mountains in

Colorado and flows 1,450 miles to the Gulf of Lower California. For a mere 20 miles it is the boundary between Mexico and Arizona, and for the last 100 miles of its course it is a Mexican stream. It drains 242,000 square miles in the United States and only 2,000 in Mexico. Its average annual flow of some 15.7 million acre-feet once seemed adequate but now will not take care of the lettuce fields, date palms, air conditioners, and highballs of the mushrooming populations of California, Arizona, Sonora, and Baja California Norte. It is a mighty—if still insufficient—resource and a bone of contention.

The natural vegetation in the border country generally is gray- or olive-colored brush or scrubby trees, except in a few river bottoms where there may be taller trees and green grass and shrubs. In some places, there are stands of Saguaro giant cactus, some more than twenty feet tall. The natural land often is poor for animals except in the stream bottoms and in the Rio Grande country, where in some brushlands deer are plentiful, with dove and quail; and some turkeys run. Mostly it is a land of darting lizards, Gila monsters, horned toads, and seldom-seen snakes. Coyotes roam and howl, pursued by ranchers who reject environmentalist claims that coyotes do not kill livestock and help preserve the balance of nature. On the plateaus real forests do not occur at altitudes under 5,000 feet, so are seldom seen on the border. They are evident nearby on the ranges and peaks of the United States and Mexico that rise out of the great North American upland.

History to 1821

Despite its harsh sun and limited water, the border country has supported human life for thousands of years. Some twenty-five thousand years ago, the seas were low, their waters locked in ice, and grassy plains lay between Siberia and Alaska. Across those plains from Siberia moved animals— many of which are now extinct—and what came to be known as the American Indians. For thousands of years humans and animals wandered south throughout the entire Western Hemisphere, the land bridge disappearing as the ice melted. A few humans settled near what much later would be the border country between Mexico and the United States.

One group in existence before 10,000 B.C. was the Clovis hunting people, named for spearheads found near Clovis, New Mexico. The moist climate of that period made the continental interior a warm land of lakes and bogs and huge mammals that the tiny humans could kill in swamps or gulleys. As the climate changed and the land turned dry and harsh, much of the big game, like the mammoth and mastodon, died out. The people became rabbit chasers and gatherers of nuts and seeds.

Eventually, maize was developed, or imported from the more advanced Indian cultures of Mexico. Squash and beans became cultivated plants. Most Indians eked out a living in the harsh environment by living in careful balance with the available water, game, and vegetation in nomadic or semi-nomadic bands. Only a few thousand lived near the later border, while a thousand or so miles to the south, in central Mexico, the great cities of Teotihuacán and Tenochtitlán, their pyramids reaching toward the sky, testified to the growth of civilization among some of the hunters who came from Asia so long ago.

In what we now call the Southwest, the Hohokam people lived near the present Phoenix, Arizona, at the confluence of the Salt and Gila rivers. They became full-time farmers and built elaborate irrigation systems before 500 A.D. Their descendants are the modern Papagos and Pimas. Northeast of the Hohokam and a bit later were the Anasazi people, out of whom came the modern Pueblos, whose great age was 1100–1300 A.D. The Pueblos spread south to the border country and then both to the east and west, similar in their adobe apartments and other culture traits, but varied in language. In eastern Texas and in far western California were more primitive Indians.

Few Indian groups had much contact with others. Travel was difficult, long before the day of such far-ranging centaurs of the plains as the Comanches. The American horse was extinct and the Old World horse was not brought by the Spaniards until the sixteenth century.

In the 1530s a few Spanish friars and conquistadores came up from central Mexico, pursuing tales of riches—the Seven Cities of Cíbola, actually poor pueblos. Friar Marcos de Niza, Francisco Vázquez de Coronado, and others explored what became Arizona, New Mexico, Oklahoma, and Kansas, finding not cities or gold, but a few poor Indians and a generally scorched and unattractive land. Interest in the area dwindled, but as Spaniards and Mexicans slowly moved northward in central Mexico, following the silver lodes to Guanajuato, San Luís Potosí, Zacatecas, and Durango, a few missionaries, traders, and primitive stockmen came to live in what now is northern Mexico. Occasionally they raided the borderlands for Indian slaves to work the mines. In 1590 they founded a village at Monterrey, 120 miles from the Rio Grande. It long remained a primitive outpost, becoming a metropolis only in the twentieth century.

A Spaniard, Juán de Oñate, finally undertook the conquest of the Zuñi pueblo-dwellers in New Mexico in 1598, investing in an expedition of some four hundred men, women, and children, eighty carts and wagons, and seven thousand head of stock. There was little Indian resistance, but the colony barely survived. Santa Fe was founded in 1609, a village in the wilderness. The Indians, apparently accepting their subordination and Christianity, secretly clung to old ways and in 1680 rebelled and pushed all whites far south to the Rio Grande. Spaniards and Mexicans return to bloodily reconquer the Zuñi from 1692 to 1696.

From northern Mexico and Santa Fe, horses got into the

hands of Indians by trade, robbery, and the growth of wild herds. Horses reached Indians on the faraway eastern fringes of the great plains and led them in increasing numbers to a wandering life in that huge area, galloping after buffalo, and dragging their tepees and other gear on long poles trailed behind "ponies." In the eighteenth century the plains Pawnees traded with Spanish Santa Fe and Taos for horses and sold them far to the east.

The scant far northern activity was of little interest to Spain or its viceroy in Mexico City—until in 1683 the Sieur de la Salle emerged at the mouth of the Mississippi River from French Canada. The next year Spain heard that La Salle had French support for movement to Texas, aimed at the Indian labor and silver of central Mexico.

Spanish indifference ended, and from 1686 to 1689 expeditions went by land and sea against the La Salle settlement, finding it abandoned at Matagorda Bay in Texas, two hundred miles north of the Rio Grande. Still fearful, Spaniards in 1690 went far to the north and founded two missions among the Asinai (Tejas) Indians on the Neches River, near the present boundary with Louisiana. But the Indians were hostile, the land unkind, and communications with Mexico poor; so in 1693 the missionaries withdrew.

In the next few years the French busied themselves near the Mississippi, then in 1713 jumped west to Natchitoches in what is now western Louisiana, founding a trading post. So Mexico City ordered action, and in February 1716 an expedition left Saltillo, about one hundred seventy miles south of the Rio Grande, with sixty-five persons, including nine friars and twenty-five soldiers—an army for this howling wilderness. It marched more than six hundred miles to eastern Texas and set up a mission and presidio (military garrison, such as it was) among the Asinais. To support that tiny, isolated position, Spaniards erected an intermediate post at San Antonio, some three hundred miles north of Monterrey and Saltillo and as far from the new outpost to the northeast. These were slender threads to bind so vast an area.

The French improved their position in 1718 by founding New Orleans and in 1719 moved out of Natchitoches to drive the Spaniards from east Texas all the way to San Antonio. Three years later an expedition from Mexico of five hundred men—a gigantic effort!—reestablished in east Texas a mission and presidios. Texas also was made a separate province, with its capital at Los Adaes (now Robeline, Louisiana), not far from the French position at Natchitoches. Then, abruptly, the warfare ceased because France was busy with a desperate duel with England for control of eastern North America. That ended in 1763 after the war in which young George Washington fought on the Virginia frontier. Spain, now allied with France, lost the Floridas to England; but France, thrust completely out of Canada and North America east of the Mississippi River by the triumphant English, ceded its western claims (Louisiana) to Spain. Clearly, Spain's position in Mexico would help the allies protect the territory against the rampaging English.

In the meantime, in the west, Spanish advancement to the north was nearly stalled by fierce Indians in the mountains and deserts, and by the fact that there was little to attract men from central Mexico. The missionary friars were stopped in the 1650s in the northwest by a loose alliance of wild tribes dominated by the Apaches. The Apaches were bands that originally came down from the north and for centuries moved about in the underpopulated lands within a few hundred miles of the present border, all the way from near the Gulf of Lower California into central Texas.

The northwestern barrier was slightly pierced in the 1680s when Jesuit Friar Eusebio Kino moved into the far northwest, living among the Pimas from 1687 to 1711 and exploring the Gila-Colorado country in the territory of the present-day United States. The Pimas were foes of the Apaches, and their temporary alliance with the Spaniards allowed Kino to survive. Missions and primitive ranches sprang up. In the 1730s a silver strike in the Arizona area, in the Altar Valley southwest of the two Nogales on the present border, brought in a few Spaniards. But the silver played out, and the Apache country remained little known and dangerous.

Far away in northern California the Russians in the eighteenth century began penetrating from their fur-trading bases in Alaska, so Spain in 1769 sent from Lower California a military expedition by land and sea under Gaspar de Portolá, accompanied by the Franciscan missionary Friar Junípero Serra. A mission and presidio were founded at San Diego, within the present-day United States, in 1769. A few other towns, presidios, and missions were set up later, from San Francisco (1776) to Los Angeles (1781). But the Spanish population of Upper California remained small because there was little to tempt the men of Mexico to make the difficult journey. The land route was laid out in the 1770s by Juan Bautista de Anza with the aid of the Yumas of the lower Colorado. But the Yumas turned against the Spaniards in 1781 and killed all they could reach, and the trail was closed and not reopened in Spanish times, which ended in 1821.

With the acquisition of Louisiana, Spain again decided it could let eastern Texas decay. This decision was not altered much when Napoleon demanded Louisiana back in 1800 and then sold it to the United States in 1803. Texas in 1820 had only four thousand Mexican settlers, and Mexico for many miles south of the Rio Grande was not much more populated. Mexicans did not go voluntarily to Texas, because central Mexico seemed more valuable and assisted emigration was too expensive in view of Spain's other defense needs. So Texas lay virtually unpeopled when U.S. citizens, led by Stephen Austin, were allowed by the newly independent government of Mexico to settle in the early 1820s.

Texas was but part of the huge paper tiger Mexico inherited from Spain upon declaring its independence in 1821.

Few Europeans lived in the enormous territory from Texas north and west below the boundary of the purchase Thomas Jefferson made from Napoleon. But in the United States, nearly forty years old in 1821, people were pouring to the west who were not much impressed by paper tigers.

Mexican-American War

Americans had been moving across the Mississippi since the Louisiana Purchase of 1803. Louisiana became a state in 1812, Missouri in 1821, and clearly other western states would follow. Frontiersmen, traders, and adventurers prowled the Louisiana-Texas border between Natchitoches and Nacogdoches, a constant threat to peace between Spain and the United States. Most settlers on the Austin lands in Mexican Texas came from southern states, and counted on using black slaves. Most were Protestants. They resisted adoption of the Spanish-Mexican language, religion, and law, justifying the fears of those Mexicans who opposed this method of providing population and revenue in a lightly held land.

Events in the United States continued to arouse these Mexican fears. In 1822 a hide trade by sea began between New England and Mexican Upper California. In 1825 the U.S. Congress authorized a commission to lay out a trail from St. Louis to Mexican Santa Fe, where the population still was small, poor, and isolated.

In the 1820s in the United States there was talk that the boundary with Mexico was not at the Sabine River, as specified in the treaty of 1821 with Spain, but farther south at another stream, even the distant Rio Grande. Also worrisome to Mexico was an alteration in the relative strengths of the nations. In 1790 the population of Mexico was 5 million, that of the United States 4 million; but in 1830 it was, respectively, 6 million to 13 million.

During the years 1826 and 1827, a few of the new settlers in Texas rose in arms to create the Fredonian Republic; although it was put down by Americans from the Austin grants, it increased alarm in Mexico City. The latter tried and failed to persuade Mexicans to move to Texas. Then in 1829 Mexico abolished slavery for all the country but found it could not enforce it in Texas. By that time there were 25,000 Americans living in the province, so in 1830 Mexico combined Texas with the state of Coahuila, with its capital at Saltillo, more than six hundred miles from northeastern Texas. Texans objected to that. Then in 1835 Mexicans decided to replace their federal system with a centralized republic—not just because of the Texas issue—and Texans believed the new system interfered with their rights. The result of accumulated fears and resentments was a rebellion in Texas and a declaration of independence in 1836.

Mexico was too weak to subdue Texas. Furthermore, urged by England and France, it became almost reconciled to the idea of an independent Texas, as a buffer against the United States. The European powers dreamed of Texas as a state reaching from the Gulf of Mexico to the Pacific, permanently restricting Yankee power. That dream was shattered by Texas preference for incorporation into the U.S.

After ten years of argument over the issue of admitting new slave territory, in 1845 Texas was taken into the Union. The ensuing war with Mexico might have been avoided if the only issue had been Texas, but Americans were moving in on Mexican claims west and northwest of there, too: traders with New Mexico; fur gatherers in the Rockies; settlers and adventurers in California; and, in the arrival of Brigham Young and his Mormon followers at the basin of the Great Salt Lake. It was a movement that Washington could not have stopped even if it had tried. The United States then had a population of 20 million (against 8 million Mexicans), and it was on the move. Furthermore, the Polk administration was openly expansionist and not conciliatory. Control of the westward movement became even more impossible after gold was discovered in California, whereupon its population in four years (1848–1852) zoomed from 15,000 to 250,000, nearly all of it located in northern California, and nearly all of it Americans. No government in Washington could have controlled that. Nor could the 5,000 Mexican residents of California. In an irony of history, the U.S. faced the same problem in the 1970s, as millions of Mexicans poured into the United States.

The Treaty of Guadalupe-Hidalgo (1848) at the end of the Mexican War set the border from the mouth of the Rio Grande to the Pacific. The Gadsden Purchase of 1853 added to the United States a narrow wedge from El Paso to the Colorado River, to incorporate some lands at a lower altitude favorable to a transportation route. Thus huge territories, some of them barely explored and scarcely settled by Spain and Mexico, were transferred to the United States.

The New Southwest

Civil War General William T. Sherman, sent to pacify the Southwest, said that if he owned Texas and Hell, he would sell Texas and live in Hell. Other Americans were more optimistic. Still, development of the Southwest involved tough problems, especially "controlling" Indians, building up trans portation, supplying water, importing population, and building mining, ranching, agriculture, and, later, commerce and industry.

Americans had long since set their Indian policy: kill, enslave, drive away, or herd them into reservations. Texans had warred relentlessly with Indians and in the 1850s refused to accept reservations set up by the U.S. government. Texans were numerous enough to implement a policy of pushing Indians out, although the warfare was bitter for decades.

There were fewer Americans in New Mexico and Arizona, and the reach was farther for the army. The most savage warfare of those areas involved Americans and Mexicans against Apaches. The latter had been forced from central Texas to the west by Plains Indians in the eighteenth century but even before then were secure in the high country of desert and mountains in the far southwest. Warring to preserve their way of life, they lived in small groups, including Chiricahuas, Mimbreños, and Mescaleros. Perhaps they never totaled more then five thousand, not including the Navajos who settled down to sheep raising, weaving, and some farming, although Navajos long plundered Spanish New Mexico and after 1848 resisted Yankee penetration of Arizona.

The Apaches hated Spaniards and Mexicans the most (and later Americans) for kidnapping and enslaving their women and children. They complained that girls were turned into whores. Like women in all Indian groups, Apache women suffered gang rapes by whites. Even Navajos in faraway Arizona were taken as slaves to New Mexico. In 1866 an estimated two thousand Indian slaves (not all Apaches) were held by whites in New Mexico and Arizona and others in Sonora and Chihuahua.

As the Civil War began, Arizona had a tiny white population. When most of the army garrisons were withdrawn from New Mexico and Arizona, the Apaches swept whites from the latter, with only Tucson remaining as a place of importance— two hundred persons. The Navajo also rose against the whites. Then American troops were sent and in 1863 and 1864 tried to exterminate the Apache. The Mexican states of Chihuahua and Sonora long had paid bounties for Apache scalps, and in 1866 an Arizona county was offering $250 for each one. The war continued, ferociously, though on a smaller scale in the later 1860s, with some cooperation between the United States and Sonora and Chihuahua. The Americans considered any war method justified, including truce violations during peace talks. Then after 1871 more conciliatory methods were tried, with a policy of reservations for Indians. The warfare decreased with reduction in the size of the Indian population. After Gerónimo's last brave and pitiful stand in the late 1880s, Indian resistance had to take other forms than warfare.

American and Mexican bandits also interfered with the development of the border areas. Natural and easy in a poor country with bad transportation and weak government were brigandage, smuggling, and cattle rustling. In 1859 the band of Juan Cortina (a sort of Mexican Robin Hood) occupied Brownsville, Texas, and provoked the Texas Rangers and the U.S. Army into pursuing them into Mexico. Cortina called on Mexican-Americans to resist abuse and on Anglos to learn to regard Mexican-Americans as brothers. Brigandage remained so much a problem that the U.S. Congress in the 1870s named an investigating commission. Mexico did not care for the doctrine of "hot pursuit," although it briefly agreed to it in the early 1880s. Then, because of economic development and the law-and-order dictatorship of Porfirio Díaz (1876–1911), brigandage declined by the later 1880s.

Development depended heavily on railroads. The mules and horses that for many years had carried the freight and passengers of the borderlands were slow and expensive. In 1857 the overland stage from San Antonio to San Diego made a trip in four weeks via Tucson. In summer it was a miserably hot and dusty ride. At all times it was a jolting experience. The railroads were essential as trunk lines for the long hauls, although stages and wagons continued for years to serve as connecting links.

By 1882 rails ran from Texas through the border country to the Pacific. In 1886 the first trainload of oranges went east from California. From 1880 to 1884 the line up the central valleys of Mexico was built—1,224 miles from Mexico City to Paso del Norte (later Ciudad Juárez), in Chihuahua, across the Rio Grande from El Paso, Texas. The short route from Mexico City to the eastern United States, through Monterrey to Laredo was ready in 1888. Other lines followed. Then, considerably later, came modern highways. The first between the United States and Mexico City, with one terminus at Laredo, opened in 1936, but most of the road links between the countries were built in the 1940s and later.

The railways were important to the growth of cattle ranching. Spanish Texas had little market. The longhorns roamed half-wild. Soldiers at presidios and vaqueros (cowboys, after *vaca,* "cow") slaughtered animals for food as they pleased. Cattlemen in Texas and what now is northern Mexico drove stock to mines in Chihuahua, Durango, and Zacatecas to feed the mining camps and turn wheels and raise hoists and pull ore-crushers. But it was too far from Texas. The sheep of New Mexico also were far from buyers, though some wool went south into Old Mexico.

The Anglo and the Mexican-Texan cowboys in Texas after the 1820s used the Mexican lariat, saddle, chaps, kerchief, pointed boots with spurs, and wide-brimmed sombrero. They used Spanish words: lasso, hoosegow, rodeo, calaboose, adobe, ranch, and savvy. The ranch owner was like the Mexican patrón, boss of the cattle realm but patriarch to his people (a distant ancestor of the Ben Cartwright of the Ponderosa later prettified on television). Markets for this cattle kingdom grew rapidly after the Civil War, when for nearly twenty years cattle moved over the Chisholm Trail, from Texas through Indian territory later called Oklahoma, to railheads in Kansas. Finally, the cattle cars came to Texas itself. Some ranches became principalities.

Water was critical to border development, and disputes were inevitable. Riots occurred in 1877 in the upper Rio Grande Valley when residents of Mexico protested that irrigation water returned to the river in New Mexico was heavy with salts that poisoned crops in Chihuahua. The United States claimed that it could use river waters in its territory as it chose, but retreated in 1906 in a treaty guaranteeing Rio Grande water to Mexico in exchange for Mexican acquiescence in construction of the Elephant Butte Dam in New Mexico. The dam's waters were mostly intended for users in the United States.

The Colorado River became a problem when a new canal in 1901 began to divert its water into the Imperial Valley of

California. Mexican protests were little heeded until the diversion proved unsatisfactory and Americans proposed an intake canal on Mexican territory. Mexico agreed, for a guarantee of half the water diverted. American use grew as southern California's population zoomed. The All-American Canal was built north of the border to divert water to southern California, and a great dam at Boulder Canyon was completed in 1936, impounding a lake and generating electricity. Increased use in the United States cut the river's flow into Mexico and polluted it with soil salts.

Mexico's protests had little impact until it found a lever, far away, in the Rio Grande basin. That was a prosperous farming region by the 1940s, with both sides of the border sending fruits and vegetables throughout the United States. Mexican dams and canals reduced the flow to the Rio Grande, thus presenting a reversal of the Colorado River dispute. Most of the Rio Grande's water in the lower river came from its Mexican tributaries, but new dams and canals in Mexico cut the flow to the main river. Texas pressured Washington for "protection," so Washington was willing to compromise. It also wanted to improve Mexican cooperation during World War II. The result was a treaty (1944) guaranteeing water to Mexico from the Colorado River and to the United States from the Rio Grande. Although amounts were not set, the principle of collaboration was.*

In the later nineteenth century some border areas enjoyed mineral and petroleum booms. Commercial agriculture continued to expand. Pink grapefruit alone created fortunes in the Rio Grande Valley. Then came manufacturing. Chambers of commerce from Brownsville to San Diego touted the cloudless skies—and the availability of power for air conditioning. The equivalent Cámaras de Comercio and Cámaras de Industria in Mexican border towns invited development. In the

---

*For more on subsequent U.S.-Mexican water disputes, see chapter 9.

U.S. the virtues of the Sun Belt became obvious to business people, tourists, and retirees—as they had been discovered long before by the armed forces. In Mexico, citizens of the border towns enjoyed higher incomes than in most of Mexico, much of it due to the exchange of goods and services between the two countries. That was important earliest on the Rio Grande section of the border, with interchange of some consequence even before Texas statehood was achieved in 1845. It came later in California, whose statehood came in 1850, but development took a long time in the southern part of the state. Growth lagged in Arizona and New Mexico, both of which left territorial status for statehood in 1912.

Mexican Revolution, 1910–1917

Border relations became dangerous during the great Mexican Revolution of 1910–1917, an eruption of rage that ended the Díaz regime, with its favors to the lords of haciendas, sale of national resources to foreigners, and disdain for peons and peasants. During this civil war many Mexicans prudently stepped over the border into the U.S. There they sometimes broke neutrality laws by helping factions back home. Some revolutionary exiles, such as Francisco Madero, who lived in Texas from 1910 to 1911, received aid from local Mexican-Americans. Also, businessmen in U.S. border towns, often owners of hardware stores, sold arms and munitions to Mexican nationals. Violence, fear, grief, and greed made a combustible mixture along the great border.

A group of Mexicans and Americans, led by the Flores Magón brothers, Mexican anarchists, invaded Lower California from the United States in November 1910. Some of the unsuccessful band members were pro-Mexican, some wanted an independent republic, others wished to attach northwestern Mexico to the United States. Civil war in Mexico encouraged such forays across the border, even though President William

H. Taft did not. The violence in Mexico led Taft in March 1911 to order mobilization of 20,000 men for border duty.

After Madero became president of Mexico in November 1911 he complained that arms and munitions for his enemies came into Mexico from the United States. Taft and the Congress made some effort to control the traffic, but it was difficult. In February 1912, however, when Pascual Orozco revolted in Chihuahua, Taft embargoed arms to the rebels while allowing sales to Madero's government.

Great civil wars always damage foreign nationals and their property. Equally inevitable, in 1912 Americans demanded that Washington provide protection. That demand was especially worrisome to Mexico because the common border made action so simple. Furthermore, historical memory and the presence of new oil fields near Tampico, made Mexicans fear a plot to seize Mexican territory under cover of preserving order.

Violence increased in Mexico when the moderate Madero was murdered in February 1913 by a group that included General Victoriano Huerta. Woodrow Wilson, inaugurated on March 4, soon tried to end arms sales to Huerta; but the border was porous and European governments declined to stop shipments by sea. Wilson took another tack by recogniz-ing the claim of Venustiano Carranza of Coahuila to be provisional head of a "Constitutionalist" government. Carranza also was accepted by the important northern military leaders Alvaro Obregón of Sonora and Pancho Villa of Chihuahua. Finally, Wilson permitted arms sales to the Constitutionalists. Huerta resigned on July 15, 1914, partly because of Constitutionalist military victories, partly because of U.S. interventions at Tampico and Veracruz in April 1914, essentially to weaken Huerta. American forces occupied Veracruz until November, despite Carranza's denunciation of the intervention, which Wilson thought he should welcome! The American president could not fathom the nationalist Carranza but finally wearied of squabbling with a leader who clearly was in the ascendant. So, on October 19, 1915, Wilson recognized Carranza's government and embargoed arms to all other Mexicans.

That led to more striking border incidents. In October 1915 Villa's army had Constitutionalist forces penned in at the border town of Agua Prieta, across the line from Douglas, Arizona. Carranza got permission from Wilson to move his troops across Texas, New Mexico, and into Arizona to reinforce Agua Prieta. On November 1, the Constitutionalist troops drove across the border and forced the retreat of Villa, who was fuming at Wilson's action. As a result, on January 10, 1916, a Villista group stopped a train at Santa Ysabel in central Chihuahua and killed several U.S. mining personnel, an action that infuriated many Americans. Carranza promised to punish the Villistas but was in no position to do so at once. The U.S. Congress on March 7 resolved to undertake armed intervention to protect Americans citizens in Mexico. On the same day Villa himself added to American outrage by leading a raid on the border town of Columbus, New Mexico. Although he was repelled by American soldiers and civilians, seventeen U.S. citizens were killed.

President Wilson, with wide backing in the United States, ordered troops into Mexico to seize Villa. On March 15 they crossed the border under General John Pershing. During the next several years American soldiers frequently chased raiders in Mexico. Civil war in Mexico just over a common border led to a state of constant actual or threatened invasion by the United States.

Carranza's reaction to the invasion (or "hot pursuit") was at first temperate, but that did not last long. Pershing could not find Villa in the wild country of Chihuahua. Before long, Mexican troops and private citizens attacked the invaders. Carranza and other Mexican leaders demanded that American troops withdraw. In June 1916 some Mexicans raided U.S. territory. On June 21 there was an ugly firefight in Mexico between American and Carranza troops. War seemed possible, though neither government wanted that. Wilson wearied of Mexican problems as Washington drew nearer to war with Germany. Finally, he pulled the troops out of Mexico and appointed an ambassador to Mexico in February 1917. Thus, more important concerns drew America's interest away from its neighbor. Years later, other issues would be decided in Mexico's favor in a similar way with the coming of World War II.

Fortunately for Mexico, political and economic conditions enormously improved between the world wars, so its border situation with an immensely stronger nation was not again dangerously complicated by disorder at home.

Border Population

Living very near the border now, in both countries, are some six million people, most of them in twenty-one twin cities divided by the boundary. The Mexican cities usually are larger than the American. San Diego-Tijuana is the largest complex, with some 1.7 million people, about half in each country, and with Tijuana growing the faster. Mexicali in Mexico has 400,000; Calexico, across the border, only some 11,000. El Paso-Ciudad Juárez have about a million, more than half of them in Mexico. The two Laredos share about a quarter-million, three fourths of them in Mexico. The growing size of the border cities has complicated problems of economic exchange and of control of illegal activity.

The growth of the Mexican cities rests in part on all conditions in a large country—some 760,000 square miles, eleventh largest in the world. Mexico has bountiful natural resources, a stable political system, and one of the best economic growth records in recent times—an average of better than 6 percent per year since 1940, scarcely matched elsewhere. If that growth rate has not created a paradise for Mexicans, the same can be said of all states in the world.

Finally, there are many Mexicans: 65 million, making Mexico the eleventh most populous nation in the world.

Mexico swarms with children, and living conditions permit them to grow up and have families of their own, so that the population grows by 3.5 percent a year, compared to less than 1 percent in the United States and the USSR. There were only 19.6 million Mexicans in 1940, but 48.3 million in 1970. It is projected that Mexico's population will be 120 million by the year 2000. At that rate, sometime in the first half of the twenty-first century Mexico will have more people than either the United States or the USSR.

Border Crossings

People and goods crossing the border now are more troublesome than past disputes over water, which is now channeled, divided, and purified by agreement. Such manipulating is harder to do with goods or people. Much of the flow of people and goods is legal, but much is bootlegged. Growing to unmanageable proportions for both countries, this flow threatens to poison international relations.

There is a constant legal flow of people, with little restraint on crossings not meant to penetrate the interior. Many Mexicans clog the crossings in the early morning to work in the United States; then late in the afternoon and in the evening the flow reverses. In addition, there are millions of crossings to buy goods or entertainment. There are some 20 million American visits to Tijuana a year, with U.S. Navy personnel flowing back and forth between San Diego and Tijuana like the tide. There also are huge American military bases elsewhere along the border. Their personnel and other Americans pour more than $1 billion a year into Mexican border towns.

Americans go south for entertainment, even though the need might seem less acute than in the past. During Prohibition (1918–1933) the legal booze in Mexico held obvious charm. Once upon a time sex for sale seemed more conveniently packaged in Mexico, but that was before the massage parlor illuminated the North American scene. For some years

Ciudad Juárez was a giant divorce mill, attracting Americans from as far away as New York. With one-day divorces, it was a pleasant way of cutting the tie. But at the beginning of 1971 Mexico closed it down as degrading to the national image.

Still, the Mexican border areas offer tequila and fine Mexican beer, bullfights, nightclubs, prostitution, souvenirs, and other goods, and the pleasure of living briefly and safely in a different culture. It is pleasant to have an "exotic" meal in Mexico, even though the border towns have become infected with a "Tex-Mex" cookery, which central Mexico disdains.

Finally, there is some pleasure in visiting Mexico in order to appreciate the familiar virtues of the "good old U.S.A."

Swelling international contact along the border, much of it illegal but openly winked at, was found by Mexico City to be a barrier to integration of the national economy. Mexicans in Matamoros, ran the writ from the Federal District, should not go to Brownsville and buy sheets made in North Carolina, but stay home and buy sheets sent from factories in Puebla; buy electric blenders made in the interior, not cheaper blenders made in Schenectady, New York.

Mexicans, however, continue to buy goods in American border towns because of their higher quality and lower price, even driving from the far interior to buy in the border marts of the United States. Since much traffic defies Mexican law, partly by bribery of low-paid officials, no one knows the total value of smuggled goods. Stores in Laredo and other American border towns could give some idea, since many advertise in Spanish and cater to customers from over the border. The traffic was so notoriously heavy by 1970 that a Mexican distillery touted its Scotch whisky (the only whisky Mexicans consider palatable) on television by showing the surprise and anger of Mexican smugglers in discovering that it was as good as contraband.*

---

*The Mexican currency devaluation of 1976 cut heavily into U.S. border sales to Mexicans, but subsequent price increases in Mexico began to make it more attractive again.

U.S. expenditures in Mexico include not only jewelery, rugs, pottery, petroleum, tomatoes, and railway cars, but the huge outlays of tourists at such interior playgrounds as Acapulco and Puerto Vallarta, and investment in commercial and manufacturing enterprises. The Mexican government encourages United States corporations to lease land in Mexico's border cities and to import raw materials free of duty as long as the finished products are exported to the United States. The lure to American manufacturers is the same as that in Hong Kong and Taiwan—cheap labor. By 1977 there were more than six hundred American plants just south of the Mexican border, assembling such items as tools, electronic equipment, and shoes. Some of America's best-known corporations thus carry jobs to Mexico—as American organized labor complains —and Mexico derives income from wages, taxes, and the sale of supplies and services.*

The Drug Traffic

Marijuana and narcotics smuggled from Mexico became a serious and much discussed problem in the 1960s and 1970s, when American use greatly increased. The issue became emotionalized as marijuana came to represent an alternative life-style which included student radicalism. People believed that marijuana introduced users to LSD, heroin, and cocaine. Drugs seemed to some Americans a cause of violent crime and of corruption, degeneration, even revolution.

Heroin and cocaine usage in Mexico is severely repressed, and in any case is too expensive for most Mexicans. Marijuana and hallucinogenic mushrooms and other plants have been confined chiefly to the religious and social rituals of small indigenous groups. But producing and exporting marijuana and heroin for the U.S. market naturally appeals to the

---

*See chapter 8 for more on economic exchange between the two countries.

cupidity as well as the real economic need of many Mexicans. They are not concerned that the traffic often is controlled by criminals from several countries.

The marijuana trade is cheapest and safest. Usage is widely accepted in the United States, and the usual penalty for possession of small quantities is on the order of a traffic ticket. Marijuana is widespread in wild form, even in Kansas and Nebraska. It is easy to cultivate and process. Users often raise it in flowerpots, a not uncommon decorative theme of the counterculture. But Mexican marijuana is better quality, much of it grown in large quantities. In northern Mexico its sale value to poor farmers in a poor land is tempting. Detection is difficult in so vast a territory. The farmer may get a ton of marijuana per acre and sell it for $3,500 in a country where the average annual income is only about $1,000. In Mexico City the ton sells for $20,000. In a city in the southwest United States, the ton retails for $30,000. Cut into kilogram bricks, the ton fetches $100,000 to $215,000. Broken down into lids (one-ounce bags), the ton sells for almost half a million dollars. So profits are high, even allowing for costs —transportation, bribes, protection, and losses to law agencies.

Such amateur American traders as students, housewives, tourists, and military personnel carry small amounts across the border—in brassieres, shoe heels, and spare tires. Body searches foul up the lines at border stations, bringing howls of protest when customs agents guess wrong. Professional smugglers, on the other hand, move tons of marijuana at a time, usually in large vehicles. Organization, speed, and bribery help them evade detection.

Heroin production and smuggling are riskier. The orange-red poppy flowers stand out more—especially from the air— than the green stalks of marijuana. Lesser social acceptance of heroin means greater efforts at control. The cost is higher than for marijuana because heroin requires more intensive cultivation, and converting the sap of the seed pods to powder requires expensive equipment and procedures. The high value tempts hijackers, with financial loss and personal injury to smugglers.

Cocaine is a South American product that merely passes through Mexico, leaving profits behind. Derived from the leaves of the coca plant of the Andes mountains, the refined product equals or surpasses heroin in value. Mexico is an entrepôt because of its well-established networks with the United States, where the demand is large.

Cooperation by Mexican authorities is one key to control. Drugs are best destroyed in the fields, before they hit the market. A sealed border would do almost as well, but that cannot be arranged without creating economic distress in both countries, and neither is willing to pay the price. Nor is either country willing to pay for the huge number of guards that would be needed to effectively patrol two thousand miles of border. They would have to be well paid to keep down bribery.

Mexican authorities, on the border and in the interior, make a considerable effort, fearful of the spread of drug use in Mexico and of the obvious crime and corruption of officials caused by the traffic. The head of the Mexican Federal Judicial Police was arrested in San Antonio in 1972 with eighty-nine pounds of heroin in his possession. Great Mexican efforts to control the growing of opium poppies and marijuana in the mid-1970s were effective, partly because the United States gave aid with helicopters and herbicides. By early 1980 the U.S. Drug Enforcement Administration noted that flows from Mexico were notably down. Of course, flows were up from other countries.

The drug traffic contributes to corruption and crime in the United States, as well as in Mexico. Border residents sometimes suffer from warfare between drug gangs. Nuevo Laredo, Laredo, and San Antonio endured street shoot-outs in 1972. The Mexican national police commandant was sent to Nuevo Laredo, only to be machine-gunned to death there. Mexican

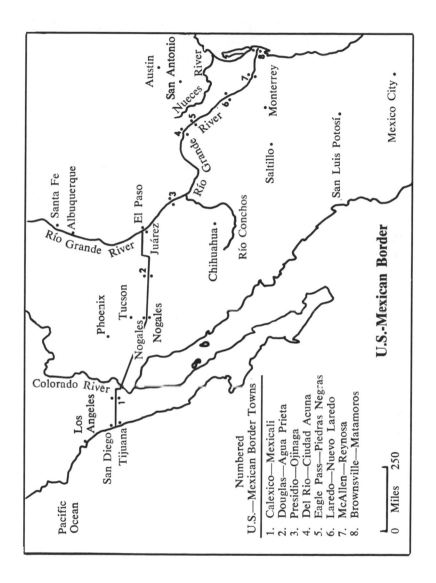

U.S.-Mexican Border

Numbered
U.S.—Mexican Border Towns
1. Calexico—Mexicali
2. Douglas—Agua Prieta
3. Presidio—Ojinaga
4. Del Rio—Ciudad Acuna
5. Eagle Pass—Piedras Negras
6. Laredo—Nuevo Laredo
7. McAllen—Reynosa
8. Brownsville—Matamoros

0 Miles 250

army units were moved into the area. Americans said it showed the poor quality of Mexican police work; Mexicans said it showed their willingness to take any necessary measures, as opposed to the feeble efforts of American agencies.

Americans jailed in Mexico, often for drug possession, get sympathy back home by complaining of brutality and crying their innocence of anything but long hair, poverty, and use of —never commerce in—drugs. It is true that Mexican police occasionally single out what they call North American "ippies," but increasing addiction of Mexicans to the youth culture makes long hair and sloppy clothes less a plain mark of just the Yankee. In any event, young people are a small problem between two large nations. Only a handful of Americans were involved in the exchange of prisoners arranged in 1977. The Americans from Mexican jails and the Mexicans from northern calabooses both went home with tales of their brutal treatment at the hands of their foreign jailkeepers.

The larger problem of drug traffic from Mexico to the United States will not much escalate because today there are so many alternate sources of marijuana and narcotics. Jimmy Jones may grow marijuana under lamps in his closet or buy hard stuff from dealers hooked into poisonous networks reaching across the oceans to Italy, Turkey, and other lands. So why take drastic measures against Mexico, when the junk merely will flow through other channels? And no one knows how to cut use in the United States, the heart of the problem. For all the talk, this is not a major issue between the United States and Mexico.

It is otherwise with the illegal flow of Mexicans across the border.

FOUR

Mexican Immigration Before World War II

During the 1840s, observers thought that Yankees would flow from Texas to the Valley of Mexico and the Isthmus of Tehuantepec and beyond. They were wrong; instead, the tide moved in the other direction, at first slowly, then with increasing force. This movement from Mexico was scarcely noticeable until the beginning of the twentieth century. By the 1920s the number of Mexican immigrants—legal and illegal—alarmed restrictionists, who had just stopped the great flow of Europeans to America. The Great Depression apparently put an end to the movement from Mexico, but World War II created pressures to begin it again. Many employers wanted Mexican labor, though the idea was opposed by organized labor and by people who thought Mexicans both unassimilable and culturally and "racially" inferior. But at the beginning of World War II neither the size of the Mexican-American community nor the likelihood of more heavy immigration much concerned the United States.

Early Mistreatment of Mexican-Americans

In 1848, even with the treaty cessions, fewer than one-half of one percent of Americans were of Mexican ancestry—

47

80,000 in a total of more than 20 million. Most of the Mexican-Americans were in Texas, and nearly all the rest in the border areas of California, New Mexico, and Arizona. The treaty gave them citizenship unless they took steps to reject it, which few did. They could not afford a move to Mexico, and the new U.S. Southwest held, for many, deep family roots, some older than those of the *Mayflower*'s descendants.

The new Mexican-Americans soon learned that treaty and law were not enough to guard their rights. They, with Negroes, were outside the American tradition of equality. They were "greasers," "half-breeds," or "Mexicans," all meaning an inferior caste. That was an Anglo view made up of bigotry, ignorance, greed, plus a potpourri of convictions "dignified" with spiritual or patriotic terms. It was a view that included, also, the common human distaste for foreign ways and faces.

These views had been evident in the English colonies. Puritans were notably intolerant. Much later, an upswelling of such passion occurred in the 1840s and 1850s as Germans and Irish, often Roman Catholics, poured into the Protestant United States. Nativism spawned rancor against the newcomers. The American Republican party, created in New York in 1843, became the Native American party. The movement slowed during the Mexican War and the hot slavery debate that led to the Compromise of 1850. Then in the early 1850s nativism flared again, festering in secret societies— like the Order of the Star-Spangled Banner—that combined prejudice and fear with political ambition. Since members denied knowledge of the societies, they were called Know-Nothings. They wanted only native Americans (not including Indians, of course) elected to office, and naturalization made more difficult for immigrants—who tended to vote for Democratic party opponents of Know-Nothings. The movement became the American party in 1855, then disintegrated in the passion of the slavery debate, many of its members going into the new Republican party.

Nativism and racism long were rife among Anglos in Texas and found new voice in a delegate to its constitutional convention of 1845:

> I shall welcome the Norwegian and Spaniard. . . . It is not these I fear. . . . But hordes of Mexican Indians may come . . . who, though able to speak the Spanish language, are but the descendants of that degraded and despicable race which Cortez conquered.*

There spoke centuries of English prejudice against Indians, and it was joined by a conviction that Spanish-American ways were corrupt and inferior. John Adams and Thomas Jefferson were two of the founding fathers who thought the cultures of Spanish and English America too different to make relations between them easy. Such attitudes killed the cry for annexation of all Mexico during the war of 1846–1848. A New York newspaper declared in October 1847 that the United States should "liberate and ennoble" the Mexicans. Others used "civilize" and "regenerate" to describe the American mission. But others doubted the possibility of "Americanizing" Mexicans. That view prevailed. With ratification of the Treaty of Guadalupe Hidalgo, the All-Mexico movement quickly dissolved.

Further annexations were also made difficult by the slavery debate. The Wilmot Proviso—that territory received from Mexico should never allow slavery—was first presented to Congress in August 1846. It was presented many times thereafter for consideration of the increasingly antagonistic sections. But the assimilation issue was at least as important in the rejection of the All-Mexico cry, as was to be true of the Philippine issue many years later.

Anti-Mexican actions multiplied in the new border states.

---

*Paul S. Taylor, *An American-Mexican Frontier* (Chapel Hill: University of North Carolina Press, 1934).

The hundred-thousand Anglos who rushed for California's gold in 1848–1850 moved to oust "californios" and foreigners from mine ownership: vigilantes threw californios off mine sites, the first California Assembly asked Congress to bar californios and foreigners from mine ownership, and Anglos tried to keep californios out of skilled jobs. Anglos violated the provision of the California Constitution of 1849 that all legislation be written in Spanish and English. They gave equally short shrift to the Treaty of Guadalupe Hidalgo articles that recognized Spanish and Mexican land titles. Both the substance and the procedures of the two legal systems were different. Between that problem and Anglo prejudice and greed, Mexicans found it difficult to defend in Anglo-Saxon courts the titles that had been written under Mexican Roman-based law.

Thus it was that in 1848 in Texas, New Mexico, Arizona, and California, an Indian was considered to be a dog, a mestizo (mixture of Indian and Spaniard) not much better, and most Mexicans thought to be one or the other. Indians in California from 1848 to 1900 declined from about 100,000 to 15,000, partly because of policies of extermination and abuse. Many Mexican-Americans in the border states were heavily Indian in ancestry, so Mexicans in the United States had a thin time of it. But poverty kept them there, and a few others came from Mexico. Most of the growth of the Mexican-American community, however, was for many years after 1848 due to natural increase, not to immigration.

Prejudice in Mexico

Anglos were not alone in their prejudice against Indians and mestizos. Upper-class Mexicans also despised their own common folk. For three centuries the Spanish system in Mexico rested on socio-racial distinction, status, and privilege. An *indio* ("Indian") was by law and custom treated as a childlike creature at best, and an animal at worst. Indians were not *gente de razón* ("fully rational humans"). They received special protection—as minors in ability and sense of responsibility—and were loaded with special burdens. Indians paid a head tax—the *tributa* ("tribute")—which was a badge of their dependent status. An Indian's legal testimony was worth less than that of a white man. Indians often were compelled to work for the upper class for pitifully small compensation. They found it virtually impossible to accumulate property, gain office outside the Indian village, obtain education, or enter the priesthood. Alienated and apathetic, they sullenly or stoically endured their inferior status, earning the reputation of being spiritless.

They did sometimes riot against abuse, but such tumults were easily crushed. Major rebellion was rare. Although such Indians as the Apache, Yuma, and Comanche were intrepid warriors, Spaniards and upper-class Mexicans declined to connect that valor with the stolid Indians in the settled parts of Mexico. Thus, unpacified and subdued Indians could be despised for different reasons, which was convenient for the egos of the ruling class.

Spaniards and Mexicans also disdained mestizos. In Mexico's colonial era, mestizos lived as closely to the Spanish mode as poverty permitted; and above all they spoke Spanish, though not well, for few were educated. They were considered *gente de razón*, but not *gente decente* ("socially acceptable"). Although mestizos often worked for Spaniards or upper-class Mexicans (creoles) as foremen, cowboys, clerks, and in other occupations, only rarely did they climb into the upper class, become *españoles* ("Spanish") of the creole version. To be sure, most upper-class Mexicans had some Indian ancestry, but the fiction of their Spanishness, or whiteness, was of no value to the great mass of mestizos. Alexander Humboldt, the great German scientist resident in Mexico just before the country's independence, wrote that everyone there was fascinated with "the fractions of European blood which belong to the various castes."

Although the new nation after 1821 abolished legal class lines, Indians and mestizos remained economically, socially, and politically an under-class. Indians, especially, still were abused. Republicanism in Mexico, nevertheless, did slightly open doors for the lower class. A few plebians rose as military leaders in a new political environment. The Spanish imperial restraint was gone, and now bullets often determined power and profit. A brave and talented Indian or mestizo could engage in that competition. Also, gradually, schools, elections, and newspapers offered opportunities. Benito Juárez, an orphaned Zapotec Indian boy of twelve who spoke no Spanish, left his shepherding in 1818, moved to the little town of Oaxaca, and went to school. Over the years he became a teacher, lawyer, and officeholder. When he was inaugurated governor of the state of Oaxaca in 1847, Indians came down from the mountains with a petition saying, "You know what we need and you will give it to us, for you are good and will not forget that you are one of us."

But Juárez could do little because the state was poor and there was no support among the politically active creoles for aid for Indians. Juárez later became a major spokesman for reform and justice, president of the republic, and heart of the national resistance to the invading French in the 1860s. The Indian Juárez, with his dark skin and high cheek bones, became the greatest name of Mexican history. But it was not easy, partly because of prejudice. When he fled in 1858 before the victorious Conservatives during the War of the Reform, a witness in Querétaro recorded that "an Indian by the name of Juárez, who calls himself President of Mexico, has arrived in this city." He fled on to the coast and to exile in the United States, later returning to fight conservatives and French invaders and becoming president again.

Among his rivals for power was Porfirio Díaz, a mestizo from Oaxaca, born in 1830. He had studied under Juárez but was chiefly a soldier-politician, common in Mexico at the time. From an early age Díaz fought in the wars of his unfortunate country—against the caudillo Santa Anna, against the Conservatives in the War of the Reform, as a general in 1863–1867 against the invading French and their puppet Emperor Maximilian of Habsburg.

Now Díaz complained that the system provided neither order nor prosperity—nor the presidency for himself. After several conspiracies and revolts, in 1876 he achieved office, after Juárez's death; and from then to 1911 he built a system of dictatorial control, known as *pan o palo* ("bread or the club")—collaborate or go under. He also built a system of economic development with foreign investment and concessions that made Mexico the "mother of foreigners and the stepmother of Mexicans."

Some of Díaz's collaborators were well-educated nation-builders, who thought him ignorant and crude, and themselves a technical and intellectual elite. Known as *científicos,* some of their views came from the positivism of sociologist Auguste Comte, which included a disdain for "old fashioned" liberal and parliamentary ideas, in favor of a "scientific"—what we would call a technocratic—social design. Their god was the idea of "progress," comparable to our notion of "modernization." Progress required that Mexico be Europeanized. The *científicos* thought Indians poor material for that, and so wanted Europeans to help build a brave new Mexico. The difficulty was that Europeans did not want to go to Mexico and compete with Indians and mestizos.

So Mexico remained Indian and mestizo. The Díaz government, however, helped keep the peons and other laborers docile and on the land or in mines and workshops. Or it took their land and forced them into slavery, as in the case of the Yaquis of the northwest. When the Yaquis tried to defend their fertile lands in the 1880s, the government subdued most of them by a savage war and the tactics of starvation. Many Yaquis were sold to plantations in far-off Yucatan, to the profit of the governor of Sonora and his cronies. Thus, Mexican and American policies were equally blind to the possibility that Indians had rights and needs of any significance.

Immigration, 1880s–1920

As opportunities grew slightly in the 1880s and 1890s, a small stream of temporary and permanent Mexican workers crossed the open border, working for mine operators, railroads, and farmers in the Southwest. New arrivals from Mexico in the growing Southwest were much fewer, however, than those moving from the rest of the United States; so no one feared that the region was being Mexicanized. The 1900 census counted some 300,000 persons of Mexican ancestry, mostly in the border area. Only 103,000 were of Mexican birth, showing that much of the growth of the Mexican-American community was due to the natural increase of the 80,000 Mexicans in the United States in 1848.

The United States had done little to restrict any immigration. Acts in the 1880s and 1890s and 1903 excluded such special classes as convicts, idiots, and anarchists. The Chinese Exclusion Act of 1882 and later extensions had a narrow effect, as did the 1907 "Gentlemen's Agreement" by which Japan agreed not to permit emigration. Bureau of Immigration personnel on the border were more concerned with stopping Europeans and Orientals from entering the United States than Mexicans.

Then, during the years 1900–20, Mexican movement to the United States quickened, with about 200,000 entering legally and more than that illegally. According to the census, the Mexican-born rose from the 103,000 in 1900 to 221,415 in 1910, and 486,408 in 1920. The Mexican influence increased also as the second-generation population grew, together with the daily and intermittent commuters in the Mexican border areas who worked in the United States and returned to Mexico at night or every few days.

Larger immigration resulted partly from economic development in the Southwest. From 1900 to 1920 California orange output rose more than 400 percent. Southwestern lettuce, cotton, and other crops increased fabulously. Just clearing the brush and trees for new fields took much rough labor. Demand for labor was so high that employers and their agents went to border towns to hire immigrants and also sent notices into the interior of Mexico. More employers realized how nearly ideal Mexicans were for their needs. They were close by, worked hard, accepted low wages and poor working conditions, and would take seasonal employment and move on when it terminated. The seasonal workers who left after planting and harvesting seasons relieved strains on the purse and conscience of Anglo employers. The low wages early in the twentieth century often meant about one dollar a day, usually less than that paid to any group for similar labor. But that was more pay than in Mexico and was often supplemented by the toil of wife and children as well. Furthermore, living costs were little more than in Mexico.

Western mines, railroads, and construction projects also depended heavily on Mexicans, who supplied over 70 percent of western railroad labor between 1900 and 1920. The railroads sowed Mexican communities throughout the West and Midwest, as workers settled along the lines they built or maintained. Mexican-American communities expanded in Los Angeles, San Antonio, and other towns not far from the border; but they also were formed or enlarged in the far interior—in Kansas City, St. Louis, and Chicago, where slaughterhouse, iron mill, and factory operators found that Mexicans worked as well as European immigrants.

Mexicans also emigrated because of worsening conditions at home. The last years of the long Díaz dictatorship saw a decline in the average person's income. Then came the Revolution of 1910–1917, with northern Mexico a principal site of combat, suffering much destruction, dislocation, and flight before marauding bands and armies. At the same time the hold of great estate owners on their workers was reduced or ended.

Although both Washington and Mexico City generally were willing to ensure the southwestern labor supply, problems arose during World War I. The 1917 Immigration and Nationality Law was America's first general restrictive measure, requiring that immigrants be literate (in some language) and that they pay an eight-dollar head tax. It caused a slowdown of Mexican immigration, but the Labor Department found ways to ignore or weaken its provisions. Temporary workers were permitted—73,000 entered legally from Mexico between 1917 and 1923. Simultaneously, southwestern employers let immigration officials know that they preferred an open border policy to lessen even the minor supervision of border crossings that was customary. So, inspections were not rigorous.

The Mexican government consented to allow its citizens to emigrate, though it could not get assurances from Washington that Mexicans would be treated fairly. Mexico was driven to this policy by the great financial losses of the Revolution and by the fact that some income from Mexican labor in the United States made its way back to Mexico. In fact, the government even aided the movement; President Carranza (1917–1920) offered free rail transportation for emigrant workers. For different reasons, the Mexican and American governments approved written contracts between employers and *braceros* (strong arms) that obligated workers to make daily deposits in a U.S. Postal Savings Bank to a total of fifty dollars. Only when the bracero returned to Mexico, could he take principal and interest back with him—and it bought much more than it would today.

Immigration in the 1920s

Given such stimuli, Mexican emigration soared. Almost 225,000 legal entrants to the United States were recorded during the 1920s and at least as many came illegally. Immigration officials, sympathetic to both immigrant and employer, did not enforce the law strictly. Another aid to immigration was completion of the railway from Guadalajara in west central Mexico to Nogales on the Arizona border. It funneled Mexicans into Arizona and especially into California. In the 1920s California rivaled Texas as a magnet for the Mexican-born, and no other state had more than a small fraction of the total.

All this accelerated movement faltered when the Immigration Act of 1924 required a visa costing $10. That, with the eight dollar head tax of the 1917 law, was too much for Mexicans (although American employers sometimes paid it for them). But the barrier was an illusion, because Mexicans merely resorted more to illegal entry. The border position offered Mexicans an advantage not available to Italians and Slavs. The porousness of the border was well known in Washington, where lack of interest in tight control left the Immigration Bureau with only a few dozen men on the border. Responding fractionally to pressure, Congress in 1924 established a 450-man border patrol for both the Canadian and Mexican frontiers! Using all 450 men to patrol the two thousand miles of border from Brownsville to San Diego would still have been ludicrously inadequate. But, of course, western employers and their congressmen wanted it to be inadequate.

The agribusiness of western America had become gigantic, feeding an industrial and urban nation. Such crops as lettuce and tomatoes took more labor than wheat, and the prosperous United States no longer was satisfied with bread, meat, and potatoes. Salad and citrus now graced tables that previously scarcely had seen them at Christmas. Western farmers, contemplating this lovely market, commanded cheap Mexican labor by enticement, inducement, advertising, political pressure, vagrancy laws, and recruitment offices. The workers came because miserable though wages, labor conditions, and living arrangements were, prospects looked worse in the slums of Los Angeles, the shacks of agricultural Texas, or throughout most of the Republic of Mexico.

The result was that of the 200,000 farm laborers in California in the 1920s, some 75 percent were of Mexican ancestry, many Mexican-born. They moved up and down the state and into adjacent states, stooping or stretching to harvest the crops and doing other rough labor. They lived in burlap tents, canvas and waste-lumber lean-to's, and brush and palm-leaf huts. Water often was insufficient and impure, ditches and holes were used for garbage and human waste, and over everything hung clouds of flies and the sour smells of malnutrition, dysentery, and despair. But the permanent communities through which they passed could almost pretend that the migrants did not exist. One of the authors can remember that as a boy in the 1920s in Banning, California, he watched at night the fires of the almond and fruit pickers down by the Southern Pacific tracks but was not allowed to go too near. So Anglo boys not only accepted the Mexican servitude—as Tom Sawyer did Negro slavery—but had little of the intimate contact with and affection for the under class that Tom had.

Most Americans knew nothing of all this. Nor did they realize that total entries from Mexico to the United States between 1900 and 1930 were on the order of three-quarters of a million. The growing immigration, though, was small in relation to the total 18.63 million immigrants who entered the United States during the same period. Americans were not much aware of people of Mexican ancestry, even though more of them moved into the Midwest.

Chicago had only 1,224 persons of Mexican ancestry in 1920, and even the great rise to 19,362 in 1930 left it a small minority in a big city. They came to Chicago in various ways, but always in response to opportunity. Some merely followed the seasonal work in sugar beet fields in Wisconsin, Minnesota, and Michigan. Many were recruited in the border towns by railway and steel companies. As news of northern jobs increased in the border areas and as new arrivals from Mexico put pressure on the labor market of the frontier, more men began to work their way north, doing railway maintenance work or odd jobs. Mostly they came from Texas, the Texans trying, ineffectually, to prevent the outflow of their cheap labor. Those leaving were mostly young men, and that caused social problems for the Mexican community in Chicago in the early days. At the same time as the early movement to Chicago, Mexicans and Mexican-Americans were in other places joining the rush to the cities that changed so much in America. By 1930 possibly 20 percent of workers of Mexican ancestry were doing at least part-time industrial work.

But changes in the numbers, residence, and occupation of people of Mexican ancestry were not striking enough to catch much attention, because the immigration "problem" for Americans was restriction of the enormous flow from Europe. That was first done by a law of 1921, as part of a quota system based on national origins. The system, adjusted in 1924 and not fully applicable until 1929, ended the ready supply of cheap European labor and, as some people thought, the undesirable effects of cultural pluralism. The quota system of the 1920s remained basic U.S. law until 1952. Its bias in favor of immigration from western and northern, as opposed to southern and eastern, Europe sparked much of the emotionalism of the immigration debate. The European stream, at any rate, narrowed drastically after 1930, and everyone hailed it happily or in sorrow as the end of a historic process.

The nations of the Western Hemisphere, however, were not included in the quota system, although there was support for that. Throughout the 1920s there were sporadic cries against immigration from Latin America, especially Mexico. The old ignorant claims about mixed blood and racial inferiority were aired. Even western supporters of Mexican immigration sometimes at least tacitly agreed but claimed that since Mexicans could easily be deported, they were the "safest" non-white group to let in, and cheap. The argument still went on in 1930 when a House bill called for Western Hemisphere quotas that discriminated against Mexico. Its sponsor spoke against the admission of "serf, slave, and peon types," a complex social question one may be sure he knew little about. Also in 1930, the Census Bureau, in an odd fashion, applied racism to Mexico. Heretofore the bureau had listed Mexicans with whites, but now it created a special "Mexican" category that listed 1.42 million for that year. The guide for enumerators in 1930 included such scientific gems as the statement that "the racial mixture" of most Mexicans is "difficult to classify," so that first- or second-generation Mexicans should be listed as "Mexican" if they were not "definitely white, Negro, Indian, Chinese, or Japanese."

The U.S. State Department in the 1920s also spoke against inclusion of the Western Hemisphere in the quota system, arguing that relations with Latin America were in a delicate state and would be damaged by inclusion in the quota scheme. The delicate state referred to was largely the result of American armed interventions in Caribbean and Central American countries. The remedy for that scarcely lay along the border with Mexico, and presumably the connection asserted impressed few persons of intelligence. What did impress congressmen and others was the pressure by powerful economic groups to include the Western Hemisphere—meaning chiefly Mexico—in the quota system. Many jewels of reasoning have come down to us on the indispensability of Mexican labor, especially in the Southwest, but none can have been more persuasive than the simple statement of the influential Congressman John Garner of Texas in 1926 that conditions in that state did not permit profitable farming without Mexican laborers.

So the new legislation left the issue of Mexican movement across the border to U.S. consuls in Mexico, who could control the number of visas issued; to the thin ranks of U.S. immigration personnel at the border; and to whatever bilateral agreements the two countries might care to make. Either the first or the third devices could be frustrated if the border remained as porous as it always had been.

Immigration in the 1930s

Unexpectedly, that porosity declined in the 1930s but not because of restrictive legislation. The change came because the Great Depression dried up the need for labor, especially labor from Mexico. There were many Anglos out of work and willing to do anything because the economy was in agony, and men sold apples on street corners; and because drought and "dustbowls" in the Great Plains drove "Okies" from Texas, Arkansas, Oklahoma, and Missouri to California. John Steinbeck immortalized in the *Grapes of Wrath* the tribulation of those Anglo-Americans; but no one dramatized the needs of Mexican-Americans, and those needs now multiplied. There were objections everywhere to giving jobs to aliens, even to Mexican-American citizens. In addition, public officials and taxpayers worried about the pressure of foreigners on public assistance agencies while the revenues of the latter were falling. Inevitably, such conditions stimulated nativism and prejudice not only in the Southwest but in other parts of the United States.

Thus, in the Southwest in the 1930s people of the Mexican community often were driven out of jobs. Visas were refused to new immigrants lest they become public charges. Then the movement went further, beginning in 1931, with deportation drives to locate and eject from the country "illegal" Mexicans. Southern California was a major focus of this xenophobia. It became hysterical and vicious, making little effort at times to distinguish between illegals, on the one hand, and citizens and permanent resident aliens on the other. Trainloads of the repatriated carried some 13,000 from Los Angeles during the years 1931–1934.

How many U.S. citizens were illegally deported or terrorized into leaving cannot be known, since the bureaucrats involved rarely bothered to count or classify the emigrés. Public officials boasted of the reduction of the Mexican population in the United States. Not surprisingly, few illegal migrants crossed the border in the 1930s and legal Mexican immigration fell to a mere 22,319 in the decade. It appeared that a combination of surveillance, abuse, deportation, and economic depression could sharply decrease the porousness of the long border. It was thought that under such conditions, the 1.5 million persons of Mexican ancestry in the United States at the end of the 1930s would possibly not be much augmented by new arrivals.*

World War II and Immigration

The conditions, however, endured only briefly. At the end of the 1930s the American economy revived as democratic governments abroad sent orders for arms and other wares, finally recognizing that militant fascism could not be appeased. Even Congress, early in 1938, agreed to more expenditures for defense. The beginning of World War II in 1939 raised demand of all sorts in the United States. It went

---

*Statistics on Mexican-Americans in the United States are a thicket of difficulties. Enumeration, classification, and publication standards vary over time. Poor people avoid and often lie to enumerators. Not all enumerators can effectively communicate with Spanish-speakers. Persons of Mexican ancestry sometimes are "hidden" in figures accumulated simply on "Spanish-speakers." Some figures are based on persons with Spanish surnames that may not be Mexican; and they include some Anglo wives but omit many more women of Hispanic ancestry married to men with Anglo surnames. Labor camps and rural huts often are overlooked, sometimes because local people try to hide them from enumerators, knowing that illegal aliens will be detected. The Immigration Service keeps only spotty records on green-card (legal) "commuters," who live in Mexico and work in the United States, or on seventy-two-hour (legal) pass holders who are not supposed to leave the border area of the United States. A 1933 spot-check by Immigration showed 52,551 intermittent and 29,963 regular commuters from Mexico to the United States. Over the years, a group of that size, furnishing people who illegally remain in the United States, could considerably influence the size of the Mexican-American community. This hints at a final, critical difficulty: the United States does not subject residents to stringent documentary checks on the model of many European and other countries, so that illegal Mexican aliens in the United States easily escape detection.

higher in 1940 as the democracies battled to survive and the Roosevelt administration helped them. American rearmament continued, and Selective Service was adopted in September 1940. By the time of Pearl Harbor in December 1941, there was an economic boom in the United States, and many men and some women had left the labor force for the armed forces. Mexican immigrants became desirable again, so employers invited and welcomed them.

They began pouring across the border, often illegally, and there was no machinery for stopping them, even if the will to do so had existed. Both governments, however, had some interest either in regulating the flow, or in showing their constituents that they wanted to do so. Mexico declined to agree to export of its citizens without guarantees that they could be protected from abuse. Increasing Mexican nationalism and past experience—deportations, prejudice, discrimination—made this a political issue in Mexico, which wanted, especially, to keep migrants out of Texas, where anti-Mexican views and acts had a virulent history.

Although illegal entrants were welcomed by American employers, they wanted a more secure system, preferably unlimited Mexican immigration. In 1941 farmers contended that they needed legal regularized imports of Mexican workers for the next season or some crops would not be harvested. Railways and other employers also wanted Mexican workers. Since employers were unable to get unlimited immigration, a temporary system seemed better than nothing. To get the agreement, Washington accepted the Mexican demand that the American federal government be the employer and handle all business and problems, including prevailing wages paid other workers and other protective measures. Mexico agreed to recruit workers and transport them to the border, where they were placed under the charge of the Farm Security Administration. The "temporary" measure went into effect in August 1942 and under one agreement or another lasted more than two decades. Since the measure was supposed to be temporary and much of the labor was supposed to return to Mexico between seasons, organized labor and nativists made only minimal objections.

The most revealing part of the agreement process, although not appreciated at the time, was the nationalism of Mexican government and press. Mexico was increasingly stable, prosperous, and confident. Leaders were less willing to permit citizens to be abused abroad. This was due to accumulated successes since the Revolution ended in 1917, especially during the administration of Lázaro Cárdenas from 1934 to 1940. Cárdenas strengthened the official party, established economic development agencies, and by greatly accelerating the communal (*ejidal*) farm program tied the peasants more firmly to the governing party and improved its reputation as a reforming and innovating force.

Another change in Mexican attitudes that had been occurring since the great Revolution of 1910–1917 was dissolution of the ancient disdain for Indians and mestizos. The official creed now was that in the Estados Unidos Mexicanos all were equally Mexicans. More, the contemporary Indian was dignified as the descendant of great civilizations of the past. Archeology became a passion. The great pyramids and exotic murals of the Maya, Tenocha, Zapotec, Mexica, and others were revealed in all their splendor—great treasures of human history and proof of the talent and achievement of the ancestors of modern Mexicans. The great Mexican revolutionary muralists celebrated Indian culture—and white depravity—on acres of walls in Mexico and, in the 1930s, at such conservative Yankee centers as Dartmouth College and Rockefeller Center Music Hall.

Nationalism and pride in the Indian heritage also were promoted by expansion of the school system, for literacy permitted more complex appeals to national sentiment. The national party and the Ministry of Education made sure that materials stressed Mexican nationalism and hopes of a greater future. The drawings in primers taught the ABCs with figures of Indian mothers making tortillas and Indian boys tending goats.

At the same time, Mexico's swelling industrial plans called for more capital, and laborers in the United States could send some back and sometimes learn useful skills as well. Finally, the peace and improved living conditions of Mexico were resulting in faster population growth in a country that already had a large number of un- and underemployed persons. Some of the pressure could be relieved by work in the United States. All of these factors played a role in Mexico's attitudes toward the "*bracero*" agreement of 1942.

Also important was the great boost Cárdenas gave to Mexican nationalism in 1938 by expropriating the foreign petroleum properties.

FIVE

Mexican Oil and Nationalism

The oil that President Cárdenas expropriated had gushed
forth in an astonishing bonanza, but it was owned and manip-
ulated by foreigners. It enriched Europeans and North Americans but did little more than corrupt Mexicans. The foreign
operators bribed Mexican officials, evaded Mexican laws, and
persuaded their own governments to coerce Mexico City.
Mexicans learned to bristle when foreigners talked about
Mexican oil; Mexicans bristled and made oil a state enterprise
in 1938. They bristled again when the United States showed
great interest in the great oil strikes of the 1970s.

Early Oil Production

Chapopotes were stinking tar pits and oil seeps where villagers went to make medicines, magic potions, and adhesive
pitch. That those seeps were potentially black gold Mexico
City knew late in the nineteenth century. The frenzy over
petroleum in the United States was reported by Mexico's
ministers in Washington and by the press and the business
community, but it was merely one more resource that Mexi-

cans could not develop. So, when foreigners came to probe around the chapopotes in northeast Mexico, the government granted permission and privileges. It was not that Mexicans were unaware of the dangers of foreign exploitation; they leapt to the eye. But Mexico needed foreign capital, so the dangers were weighed against the advantages. Thus, the dictator Porfirio Díaz (1876–1911) promoted economic modernization by favoring foreign capital, which poured into Mexico, especially from Britain and the United States.

Among the attractions were changes in 1884, 1892, and 1901 in the mining laws—from the Roman system of reposing subsoil rights in the state, to be doled out on concession, to the Anglo-American system of giving landowners mineral rights also. Britons and Americans who went into mining and petroleum exploration in Mexico after 1892 believed that the law had achieved perfection, and conveniently forgot that some countries accepted the Roman theory as socially desirable, so that a barren plain bought at sheep pasture prices could not confer mineral fortune upon a merely lucky owner.

At the time Díaz made these concessions, some Mexicans criticized the lack of controls and the excessive privileges for foreigners that were part of the system. That was a natural reaction, and it had some small effect in the nationalization of part of the railway system late in the Díaz years. But fundamentally, nascent nationalism was no match for foreign capital and its allies in Mexico before the great revolution of 1910–17.

In the 1890s American and British interests became active in Mexican petroleum exploration. Edward L. Doheny of the United States and Weetman Pearson (Lord Cowdray) struck it rich just after the turn of the century. They were bitter rivals, unscrupulous in their dealings with each other and with Mexicans, and prone to bring their home countries to their support. At first, however, it was scarcely necessary to beg diplomatic intervention, since the Díaz government was generous to the companies.

Tampico on the northeast Gulf coast was a boom town of the new industry. The town—17,569 population in 1900 and 44,822 in 1921—sat at the mouth of the Pánuco River as it emptied into the sea. It was tropical, hot and steamy, dirty, pest-ridden, isolated, ugly, and generally primitive. Crude and specialized labor poured in from abroad and from the adjacent countryside.

Peasants in rough off-white drawers and shirts, straw hats, and sandals rubbed shoulders with tool-dressers from Texas, accountants from London, bar owners from Mexico City, and whores from all over. At one time there were some five thousand foreigners in the seamy little tropical town. Most of the oil was produced from a strip running about seventy-five miles south of Tampico. The companies dredged the bar at Tampico and built an intercoastal canal south from the town into the oil fields and moved oil by barge. It was stored at Tampico in wooden tanks and in artificial lakes and filled the air with the smell of tar. Ships came for oil and brought food, equipment, and luxuries.

Each company had a narrow gauge railway from Tampico to the fields. There also was a Mexican national rail connection with the interior, but it was slow and inconvenient. Road transportation scarcely existed, although Doheny was a pioneer in selling his product for road paving.

Mexico did what it could to extract benefit from the petroleum industry through taxes (low), bribes, and the conversion of many Mexican locomotives to petroleum. Blackmail by local political bosses (*caudillos* or *caciques*) was commonly used to ensure supply routes, protect workers in the bush, and prevent theft or sabotage of installations. But Mexicans in government and private enterprise were poorly trained, unorganized, and left all alone to deal with the international petroleum giants, by now well equipped to repel the feeble efforts of underdeveloped countries.

Mexican oil production rose from an insignificant amount in 1901 to 12.5 million barrels in 1911, and much more thereafter. Most of it was exported. With world petroleum consumption constantly rising, Mexico's prospects for large oil profits seemed rosy.

Although to the developed nations Mexico in 1910 never had seemed more stable and prosperous, a few intellectuals and dissident politicians there were planning revolt and the masses of peasants and laborers were quiescent only under the lash. When the dissatisfied toppled the old regime by violence in late 1910 and early 1911, the country fell into a series of civil wars as leaders, interests, and ideas competed for control of a country more than three times the size of France, though with only 15 million inhabitants.

Foreigners in Mexico suffered much destruction of their property as well as injury and death. No government was firmly in control of the country from 1910 to 1917, so that foreign interests could not be well protected. Furthermore, it often was uncertain where protests from abroad could most effectively be lodged. The foreign oil operators naturally feared damage to their interests in the northeast. At the beginning of the movement against Díaz, the British suspected that the United States was aiming at a protectorate over Mexico, something London had feared for nearly a century. Although that view later was shown to have been erroneous, at the time it stimulated British fears of danger to all their holdings in Mexico. A report circulated that the revolutionary Francisco Madero received financing from Standard Oil Company, with the aim of damaging British petroleum interests that were favored by the Díaz regime. That report was never proven. Possibly it sprang up almost spontaneously because ruthlessness was normal—and probably necessary—in international oil rivalry.

As events proved, the oil companies were less affected by the Revolution than they feared. Their relative isolation in the Tampico-Tuxpan area was an advantage. It was remote from the large-scale military activity of the times. It was difficult for the armies that took and retook Mexico City, more than two hundred miles away, to levy tribute in the petroleum fields. Much of the time the oil area was controlled by Manuel Peláez, a regional leader with his own army and whose family held big estates in the state of Veracruz. With little zeal for social reform but a large appetite for money, Peláez was happy to sell protection to the oil companies. Even when a supposedly national government controlled the town of Tampico, the producing oil wells were in the back country, which was controlled by Peláez.

Under these conditions, oil production continued to rise, spurred by the advances of the automotive age and by World War I. Mexican oil helped fuel the allied fleets. The 12.5 million barrels of production in 1911 became 193 million by 1921, by which time Mexico was the world's second largest producer (after the United States), turning out a quarter of global production. Mexico held that second position from 1919 to 1926. The world needed oil; various Mexicans needed revenues from oil, which was mostly exported; and virtually no one was interested in the control of foreign enterprises in a time of civil war.

U.S. relations with Mexico during the great revolution were profoundly disturbed by many issues but little affected by the oil industry. That was not the issue, for example, in April 1914, when American sailors in Tampico were briefly arrested by soldiers of the forces of Victoriano Huerta, president in Mexico City, but far from ruler in all the country. The administration of Woodrow Wilson seized on the incident as a means of putting pressure on Huerta. Wilson, with good reason, regarded Huerta as the murderer of his predecessor, Madero.

The absurd squabble over the sailors at Tampico quickly escalated into a large dispute, and in the course of a few days the United States had landed troops at Veracruz. There they killed some Mexicans and remained in uncomfortable possession of the main port of Mexico until November, long after Huerta had fallen.

The Mexican Revolution went on and on thereafter, with the forces led by Venustiano Carranza gradually winning, so that Wilson faced a chief executive in Mexico that he liked little better than Huerta. Carranza's "fault" was that he would take no orders or suggestions from Wilson or accept any U.S. intervention in Mexico. But Wilson's unhappiness at the rise of Carranza was muted by American involvement in World War I and the peace thereafter. Mexico now seemed a sideshow to Wilson and most Americans.

Revolution and Foreign Producers

There were a few Americans, however, including executives of the oil companies, who thought Mexico more than a sideshow. That was founded first of all on the fact that various revolutionary leaders, including Carranza, occasionally issued reform decrees that seemed to threaten private property in general and foreign property in particular. That concern became vastly greater in 1917 when a constitutional convention produced a document providing for severe restraints on private enterprise and foreign property owners.

The Mexican constitution promulgated in February 1917 was socially and economically the most radical in force in the world. It gave a social definition to property, gave organizational and social rights and benefits to organized labor, and contained much nationalism on political and economic subjects. The national government was given control of subsoil riches, agricultural estates were to be broken up and village communal lands enlarged, foreigners were not to own land within sixty miles of the frontiers or thirty of the seacoasts, aliens acquiring land had to promise to abide by Mexican law and forego appeals to their home governments. There were extensive provisions authorizing labor unions, the right to strike, employers' liability for accident and disease, minimum wages, time limits on work, child labor reforms, and many other matters.

With promulgation of the Constitution of 1917, and especially after the fears occasioned by the faraway Russian
Revolution of 1917, many supporters of private enterprise in
Mexico and elsewhere began inveighing against "Red Mexico." That was a cry heard frequently for more than two decades, and was a favorite charge of spokesmen of the foreign
oil companies in Mexico.

Although President Carranza, inaugurated in May 1917,
was a conservative on many subjects, he was a strong nationalist. In April 1917, as provisional president, he put a 10
percent tax on oil production. Then in June he refused drilling
permits for leases acquired after February 5, when the constitution went into effect. From then until the end of his administration in 1920, Carranza issued other decrees that
increased national revenues from the oil companies and
threatened their leases. But because Carranza's policy was
somewhat ambiguous and because production was needed
during World War I, the oil companies protested but kept at
work.

President Alvaro Obregón (1920–24), the greatest military
commander of the Revolution, came to office as the United
States was suffering from the "Red Scare" of the postwar
years. This search for communists in America reinforced the
claims of those—including oil company spokesmen—who said
that communism must be put down in Mexico. The United
States refused to recognize the administration of Obregón. That
was a powerful and frequently efficacious weapon when used by
a great power against an underdeveloped and unstable country.

Although nonrecognition was intervention in Mexican affairs, Obregón swallowed his resentment. He needed recognition to avoid the belief among domestic opponents that revolt
might be supported by Washington; and he needed it internationally for credits to rebuild war-wrecked Mexico.

Obregón tried to reassure the United States with promises,
but Washington feared any Mexican agreement less binding
than a treaty, possibly overestimating the inviolability of the

latter. Obregón in 1921 and 1922 had the Mexican Supreme Court declare that if the owners of oil leases had performed a "positive act" to develop their properties before the constitution went into force, they were ensured possession. The smaller oil companies and other business interests were largely in favor of acceptance of this assurance, but the State Department held out.

The problem was then taken to the Bucareli Conference in Mexico City, May–August 1923. Agreements were reached on a number of matters unrelated to oil, and on the latter Mexico offered a "gentleman's agreement" to adhere to the doctrine of positive acts. With that, the United States recognized the Obregón government. Mexico, of course, considered that it had been coerced, yet it was a good guess that some future government would argue that such an agreement need not be honored.

Although the Bucareli agreements helped secure a friendly U.S. government attitude during the Adolfo de la Huerta rebellion in the winter of 1923–1924, the leaders of the Mexican Revolution perceived significant American business support for the conservatives supporting the rebellion. The nationalistic distaste of the leaders of the Revolutionary faction for foreign business thus was further stimulated.

At the same time, the foreign oil companies were converting their leeriness of the political climate in Mexico into a drastic decision to damp down production there. It was easy to do that because other oil producing countries (notably Venezuela) were coming on, where political conditions were more favorable—that is, local nationalism was feeble. That was the sort of global decision the oil giants could make and against which the underdeveloped country—in this case, Mexico—ordinarily had little defense.

The Plutarco E. Calles administration (1924–1928) did little to reassure the petroleum companies. Calles supported organized labor in a way that frightened all private enterprise operating in Mexico. Businessmen exaggerated the immediate consequences to themselves of Calles' labor policies, but they were right in interpreting them as portending a long-term increase in the bargaining power of labor.

In December 1925 Calles had Mexico's congress pass a petroleum law that declared possession of oil holdings acquired before 1917 would be limited to a total of fifty years. Since this violated the Bucareli agreement, various U.S. officials, private enterprise spokesmen, and journalists protested. But President Coolidge and the American public were against intervention.

State Department officials generally were disillusioned with American interventions in the smaller Caribbean countries since 1904. During most of the years of controversy in Mexico, 1917–1938, the petroleum companies were dissatisfied with the State Department's views on the Mexican situation. Nor were the companies happy about U.S. banks, which preferred compromise with Mexico rather than confrontation, so that they could get some return on defaulted bonds. The State Department quite properly concerned itself with the totality of American interests rather than with single interest groups. It is not true, as the legend has it, that the State Department jumped when Standard Oil yelled, "Frog."

In the summer of 1927, in an effort to calm various disputes with Mexico, Washington sent Dwight W. Morrow to Mexico as ambassador. Morrow proved a brilliant choice and helped quiet Mexican fears. President Calles thereupon helped persuade the Mexican Supreme Court to reaffirm in November 1927 the doctrine of "positive acts." Then Calles had the petroleum law altered to incorporate the court decision by January 1928. After that, the State Department in Washington announced that oil problems now would be left to the Mexican courts. That was what the Mexicans wanted, but it was far from the desire of the oil companies.

The companies did not abandon Mexico, but they did not lavish attention on it. From the peak production of 193 million barrels in 1921, Mexican output declined to only 33 million in 1931. A small rise occurred in the later 1930s, but, as it turned out, the production record of 1921 was not to be equaled until 1973!

The Expropriation of 1938

From 1928 to 1934, Calles was conservative boss of Mexico, managing three successive presidents of the country. During that period, about two-thirds of the oil companies received government confirmation of their holdings, although all of them disliked the very theory of reconfirmation. The six-year lull in the petroleum fight ended with the 1934 election of Lázaro Cárdenas to the presidency.

The new president, inaugurated in 1934, was intent on reform of all sorts. His administration took a stronger line on most of the revolutionary aims, including foreign holdings in Mexico. It very soon ended issuance of confirmatory petroleum grants. It also created Petróleos Mexicanos (PEMEX) as a state oil enterprise, an action that coincided with a vast extension of the communal ("ejidal") farm system. Both acts seemed clearly socialist to international and domestic private enterprise.

Cárdenas also greatly increased labor organization and improved its position in the political process, integrating the unions into a revised national party. In early 1936, as a part of the improvement of organized labor, various unions (sindicatos) joined in the Petroleum Workers' Union of the Mexican Republic (STPRM). This was part of the huge new national labor organization Cárdenas put together—the Confederation of Mexican Workers (CTM)—under the direction of the left-leaning Vicente Lombardo Toledano.

STPRM later in 1936 sent to the oil companies a contract to govern the entire industry. That sort of industry-wide collective bargaining conformed to the Mexican Labor Code of 1931. The oil companies rejected it because they preferred to deal with workers as part of a fragmented labor system. The

American companies also rejected it because at the same time new national unions in the United States were fighting for industry-wide bargaining. American private enterprise considered itself under siege.

The contract drawn up by STPRM in 1936 was offensive to the foreign oil companies for other reasons as well. It demanded the closed shop, inclusion of office workers in STPRM, higher wages, strike pay, double pay for overtime, paid vacations, and other benefits. The companies did not want to agree to those things in Mexico, nor did they want news of such heresies to reach Venezuela and other producing "colonies."

Before the industry could be disrupted, Cárdenas in November 1936 imposed a six-month cooling-off period. The companies then agreed to industry-wide bargaining and contracts and some increases in compensation, but the concessions were not enough for STPRM. The union in mid-1937 obtained government approval of definition of the dispute as an "economic conflict." The law considered that to be a condition requiring government intervention to arbitrate and then make and enforce a decision—not a pleasing prospect to the companies.

It meant that the Cárdenas regime appointed a Federal Board of Arbitration and Conciliation, more of the government intervention that private business so much lamented. The experts used by this board declared that American companies made much higher profits in Mexico than in the United States, thus they were exploiting Mexican workers. That was something that Mexican nationalists believed of all private enterprise in Mexico.

There followed the expectable dispute over profits. In December 1937 the Federal Board ordered wages increased by 27 percent, a forty-hour week, office personnel included in the union, and various fringe benefits. The companies took the matter to the Mexican Supreme Court.

In the United States, the oil companies and supporters tried to pressure the federal government and met with little success, partly because the country had an increasing interest in good relations with Mexico, and also because of the rise of fascist Germany, Italy, and Japan. It seemed to some leaders that the world faced an uncertain and dangerous future.

The Mexican Supreme Court in March 1938 rebuffed the oil company pleas, whereupon the companies raised their wage offer but coupled it with demands that no more should be requested. When no agreement was reached, the Board of Arbitration declared the companies in "defiance" (*rebeldía*), a state that permitted worker control of private enterprise. That led the largest oil producer, "El Aguila," a subsidiary of Royal Dutch Shell, to consider capitulation; but it was persuaded by the American companies not to give in.

The latter, however, had badly miscalculated the force of the new Mexican nationalism. It also had overestimated the willingness of the American government and people to pull business chestnuts from overseas fires. It was a period in which Roosevelt's New Deal had promoted harsh opinions of the selfishness of large corporations. And the fascists abroad had arms in their hands, more worrisome than wage disputes in Mexico.

The result was that when President Cárdenas, on March 18, 1938, declared the nationalization of Mexican petroleum, the official U.S. response was only a tepid disapproval. Since Cárdenas promised compensation to the oil companies, many official and private groups in the United States could accept the expropriation as legal. The British government inveighed against the seizure as improper, and Mexico broke relations with London in May 1938.

The oil companies themselves did all in their power to punish Mexico economically. They had a number of weapons, including control of tanker fleets, distribution systems, and oil production equipment. They managed to stop U.S. Navy purchases of oil from Mexico. They urged American tourists not to go across the border. Mexico compensated to some extent with increased relations with Italy, Germany, and Japan—a development worrisome to many American leaders.

Negotiations between Mexico and the companies made no headway immediately after the expropriation because the companies refused to yield, still fearful of the effects in other lands. A minor company, Sinclair, did conclude an agreement with Mexico in 1940, renouncing most of its claims.

In April 1940—with World War II some months old—U.S. Secretary of State Cordell Hull demanded arbitration, which Mexico rejected as intervention in her domestic affairs. But the wars raging in Europe and Asia quickly reduced the interest of Washington in Mexican petroleum. Furthermore, Mexico took an antifascist stand that coincided with that of the United States, which was pleasing. In April 1941 a treaty permitting aircraft of the two countries to use each other's airfields was indicative of a new atmosphere and new interests. Global developments made oil rights shrink in perspective. A number of other developments signified the growing rapprochement. The United States also found new Mexican President Avila Camacho (1940–1946) easier to deal with than Cárdenas.

Heavy pressure to negotiate the oil dispute found no support in the companies but much in the U.S. government, with the result that at the end of 1941 Washington signed an agreement with Mexico, accepting a system whereby experts would decide on the value of U.S. oil properties in Mexico. That left the companies out of the settlement process and opened the way to other agreements with Mexico on land claims, silver purchases, credits to Mexico, and improvement of trade relations. Most of this was achieved by the time of Pearl Harbor (December 7, 1941) or soon thereafter. The petroleum companies thus were left behind by history.

The Mexican and American experts easily agreed that the company claims were excessive, and an agreement of April 1942 set a value of $23.9 million, which was paid off by 1949. No doubt the companies had made large—possibly excessive—profits during their short tenure in Mexico, but they certainly got a meager terminal agreement. The new nationalism and government organization in Mexico had proved too much for the huge multinationals.

Problems of the State Monopoly

The nationalization of oil was immensely popular in Mexico, largely because it involved a swipe at the foreign devils, though a minority approved it also out of anticapitalist sentiment. Furthermore, it appealed to national pride in general, and together with other Cárdenas economic measures built confidence in the capacity of the country to develop by its own efforts. It gave a big lift to nationalism, and the sentiment of nationalism was the engine most potent for the mobilization of common efforts and the acceptance of change and sacrifice for the general good.

Expropriation and nationalization of oil did involve sacrifice. Most Mexicans, of course, did not understand the economics of the matter and supposed vaguely that with the ousting of foreigners from petroleum all its magic inhered automatically to Mexico. There was considerable woolly belief that now it did not cost anything to produce petroleum products.

A few Mexicans knew better. Mexico could not keep up exploration and open new wells and fields without outside capital and technical aid; for some years those proved hard to come by. Nor could Mexico easily keep up production from the existing wells and the distribution of its products. Nor could it easily market surpluses abroad—if it had any—without the aid of the petroleum giants. Finally, Mexico would find it difficult to alter the character of the petroleum system to meet changing needs as the country industrialized.

Mexico found it difficult to build up production, which only reached 43.4 million barrels in 1941, 78.8 million in 1951, 116.8 million in 1961, 177.3 million in 1971, and in 1973 reached 191.5 million, about the production of 1921. Building managerial and technical staff took time, and capital was limited. Mexican credit abroad was poor for some years, so that PEMEX had to live too much off its own domestic sales. There was little surplus oil for export, and that was partly because of the cry in Mexico that oil was a "nonrenewable" natural resource, not to be depleted at a "loss" to sell to foreigners.

The efficiency of PEMEX never was easy to determine. Establishment politicans claimed marvels for it, critics muttered about incredible mismanagement. The data, unfortunately, were not good enough to permit certain judgment. It was clear, however, that PEMEX activity increased, production rose, its personnel grew more numerous, and its budget soared. It kept Mexico reasonably well supplied with fuel oil and gasoline, although after 1957 Mexico became a net importer of petroleum. Mexico also went into petrochemicals, with PEMEX in 1958 being granted a monopoly of basic development of the industry. Much secondary petrochemical production was done under license by private companies, with their stock owned at a minimum 60 percent by Mexican nationals.

PEMEX grew to meet the demands of electricity production and industrial uses, both of which rose enormously during World War II and thereafter. Petroleum products were needed to pave the huge highway system that was built in those same years. And on those highways rolled more and more buses, trucks, and passenger cars, which, in the 1960s and 1970s, were chiefly manufactured in Mexico.

These roads and vehicles served by PEMEX helped reduce the ancient isolation of the Mexican village and the regionalism of the country. It was a boon to the public and a big help to the governing party and the state apparatus, including the army and police.

Not only was PEMEX a huge enterprise, but it gave the state much leverage with private enterprise because the latter depended on it for supplies. As PEMEX grew, the remaining bits of private foreign and domestic activity in the petroleum industry dwindled in significance. Most of the foreign element was liquidated by the 1950s. Mexico had tamed (at some cost) the multinational oil companies long before OPEC took a hand.

The PEMEX distribution system grew with the rest. Green-painted PEMEX *gasolinerías* sprang up by the thousand, operated by private concessionaries but required to sell only PEMEX gasoline. Fleets of gasoline and diesel fuel tank trucks rumbled down the new highways. Tank ships scarcely were needed, since PEMEX exported so little.

One of the most interesting aspects of the growth of this giant was the pricing policy of the federal government. It required PEMEX to keep the cost of fuel low. This favor to consumers especially impressed the public because it helped subsidize low bus fares and cheap gasoline for private cars, and diesel fuel and gas for the mushrooming private trucking and passenger bus industries. The directors of PEMEX, on the other hand, grumbled to their fellows in government that they were not permitted to accumulate enough capital for expansion and often had to pay heavy interest on borrowings for investment.

The New Oil Bonanza

That pricing policy was going to be abandoned in a time of crisis in the administration of President Luís Echeverría. During his tenure, Mexican petroleum production began to fall further behind domestic demand, so imports increased. Unfortunately, that occurred just when Arab and other Third World producers erected the great OPEC cartel and quadrupled the price of their oil. Mexico paid $124 million for oil imports in 1972, but $382 million in 1974, under the OPEC dispensation. It was clear that along this road lay disaster.

This was especially the case because from 1974 to 1976 production in the total Mexican economy declined to the point where it was not keeping up with population growth. That occurred in a country accustomed to annual per capita increases in national production.

Echeverría also chose to permit high imports of all sorts of supplies for the industrial plant he was so intent on fostering at a faster pace than the country could afford. He financed this extravaganza with increased foreign borrowing. The external debt rose from $2.2 billion at the end of 1967 to $9.5 billion in 1974 and $20 billion in 1976, by which time debt service required $4 billion a year. Private investors lost confidence, and the government raised public credits. That added to an irresistible pressure on prices and destroyed Mexico's twenty-year immunity from that common malady of developing countries—inflation. Finally, in August 1976 Echeverría devalued the peso. It had to be done, but the deed was met by a fury of fear and criticism. Echeverría left office in December with his reputation in shreds.

But he had made one decision not long before that promised a way out of the dilemma of need for more investment capital while the economy was deteriorating. He abandoned the policy of freezing prices at an artificially low level. The result was greatly increased PEMEX revenues, and they were used to increase production and search for new reserves.

The results of this were not evident to the public until after the inauguration of President José López Portillo in December 1976. Proved reserves of hydrocarbons (oil and natural gas) went from 5.56 billion barrels at the end of 1970, to 11.16 billion at the end of 1976, 16.8 billion by the end of 1977, and more than 40 billion at the end of 1978. There were rumors—possibly founded in part in hopes or political tactics —that reserves ultimately would exceed 200 billion barrels, topping the fantastic reserves of Saudi Arabia.

Furthermore, by the beginning of 1979 actual production of crude was up to an annual rate of about 511 million barrels, far beyond the once-fabulous year 1921. Much of the new production was going to the United States, with beneficial effects on that country's strategic position and with happy results for Mexico's threatened financial position.

So many problems between Mexico and the United States that loomed large from the 1950s to the early 1970s took on a new hue as well as new dimensions—or at least both countries hoped so. Even floods of illegal immigration to the United States could be nearly dammed, diverted, accepted, or compensated for to please the oil colossus south of the border.*

---

*See chapter 8 for more on recent developments in Mexican oil and natural gas.

SIX

A "Flood" Of Mexicans

The hope of an oil flood from Mexico came to the United States at a time of fear that America was "drowning" in a "flood" of Mexican immigrants. Emotional cries arose on both sides of the border. A Mexican population expert said in 1977 that President Carter's ideas on curbing immigration were "unfriendly," "unilateral," and insensitive to Mexico's economic situation, which required emigration as a safety valve. That statement made some Americans gasp. The *New York Times* retorted that "obviously" the United States could not be a safety valve "forever." The recorded history of the heavy legal and illegal movement of Mexicans into the U.S. from World War II to the 1970s was ransacked by each side, which hoped to prove the other's broken commitments, ingratitude, inhumanity, greed, irresponsibility, social and cultural prejudice, and failure to act like a good neighbor. The issue threatened to become an unmanageable monster.

Numbers and Categories

So, by an irony of history, what once in the nineteenth century seemed an irreversible tide of Anglos into Mexico, in the twentieth became a great flow in the opposite direction.

How great was the flow? No one knew. There were estimates and guesses, based on fragmentary, ambiguous, and invented statistics. Those who came with "green cards," giving them permanent residence with the option of naturalization, were a minority of the migrants. From 1950 to 1970, some 750,000 Mexicans obtained that visa, an average of about 37,000 per year. In the 1970s a new law limited that group to a maximum of 20,000 annually. By the end of the 1970s nearly a million Mexicans had such cards.*

Mexicans let in as temporary labor comprised a much bigger group: more than 3 million from 1942 to 1964. Many "temporary" contract laborers from Mexico stayed illegally in the States. Some brought families from Mexico. Others married in the United States. Regardless of the citizenship of the parents, children born in America were citizens.

Other Mexicans had tourist or student passes. Hundreds of thousands of others had "white cards" as "legal visitors," permitting a stay of three days within twenty-five miles of the border. Others were simply allowed to cross for the day, shopping or pleasure-bound from one border town to its American sister. But a trip from Nuevo Laredo, Tamaulipas, across the bridge to Laredo, Texas, often turned into a trip to find a job in Chicago or Milwaukee. Daily border crossings by Mexicans and Americans constantly rose. By the late 1960s they averaged more than 300,000 (well over 100 million a year); in 1975 they averaged 868,000 a day!

Even legal aliens in the U.S. lived under a bewildering variety of statutes. In 1977 the Immigration and Naturalization Service (INS) stated that there were seventeen types of alien registration cards held by more than 4.5 million persons. There is no restriction on non-immigrant visas in nearly thirty categories of visitors, which last from several weeks to a year. Competition for such visas is swamping American consular offices in many countries.

---

*About 3 million persons of other nationalities also had such cards.

In the United States, illegal Mexican aliens far outnumbered legal ones. Sometimes they arrived surreptitiously, often with aid from smugglers. A border of 1,945 miles made it difficult to control illegal crossings.

How to estimate the Mexicans illegally in the United States? One way was by INS reports of Mexicans caught illegally here. In the 1950s more than 3 million Mexican aliens were deported because they were illegally in the United States. INS declared that 1.017 million were detected in the year ending September 1977 and that that was the highest since 1954, when 1.092 million were apprehended.

Most of those apprehended were deported. Did that mean that the total pool of illegals from Mexico was being reduced? Few believed that. Deportees slipped back easily.

Then how many entered illegally each year from Mexico? No one knew. The INS guessed that 5.6 million Mexicans entered illegally between 1942 and 1967. In 1978 it guessed that there were "only" one-half million to 800,000 illegal entries a year from Mexico. Furthermore, on a number of occasions in recent years the INS had declared that it rounded up a high proportion of illegal entrants from Mexico at the time of crossing or within three days thereafter. More than a million illegal aliens were apprehended in 1979 by the INS, continuing the steady rise in such arrests. The proportion, alas, was specified in 1974 by the INS as 20 percent of the illegal Mexican entries it estimated for that year, and for 1977 the estimate rose only to 25 percent.

Illegal aliens from Mexico sometimes were discussed as part of a general problem, and then the figures were even scarier. In the 1970s the INS estimated as many as 12 million and as few as 4 million illegal aliens were in the country. In 1977 its estimate was 8.2 million. But no one really knew.

Census figures were not very helpful. The 1970 enumeration reported 4.5 million Mexican-Americans, compared with about 1.5 million at the end of the 1930s, when the big migration was thought to be finished. Even the Census Bureau de-

cided that the 1970 figure was too low. Other estimates in the
1970s put the Mexican-American population at between 6.5
million and 9.6 million, some portion residing illegally in the
country.

The illegal alien issue heated up in 1980 in connection with

Table 6.1

Legal Immigration from Mexico to the United States,
1900–1973

Year	Total Immigrants	Year	Total Immigrants	Year	Total Immigrants
1900	237	1926	42,638	1952	9,600
1901	347	1927	66,766	1953	18,454
1902	700	1928	57,765	1954	37,456
1903	528	1929	39,980	1955	50,772
1904	1,009	1930	11,915	1956	65,047
1905	2,637	1931	2,627	1957	49,154
1906	1,997	1932	1,674	1958	26,712
1907	1,406	1933	1,514	1959	23,061
1908	6,067	1934	1,470	1960	32,084
1909	16,251	1935	1,232	1961	41,632
1910	17,760	1936	1,308	1962	55,291
1911	18,784	1937	1,918	1963	55,253
1912	22,001	1938	2,014	1964	32,967
1913	10,954	1939	2,265	1965	37,969
1914	13,089	1940	1,914	1966	45,163
1915	10,993	1941	2,068	1967	42,371
1916	17,198	1942	2,182	1968	43,563
1917	16,438	1943	3,985	1969	44,623
1918	17,602	1944	6,399	1970	44,469
1919	28,844	1945	6,455	1971	50,103
1920	51,042	1946	6,805	1972	64,040
1921	29,603	1947	7,775	1973	70,141
1922	18,246	1948	8,730		
1923	62,709	1949	7,977		
1924	87,648	1950	6,841		
1925	32,378	1951	6,372		
				Total	1,736,576

Source: Stanley R. Ross, ed., *Views Across the Border: The United States
and Mexico* (Albuquerque: University of New Mexico Press, 1978),
p. 166.

the decennial census. States with many undocumented aliens wanted them counted; others did not. At issue was apportionment of seats in the House of Representatives and the size of federal aid to states and localities, based on population. The statistical fog was made denser by figures on Spanish

Table 6.2
Illegal Mexican Aliens Apprehended
and/or Deported, 1924–1973

Year	Number of Persons	Year	Number of Persons
1924	4,614	1950	469,581
1925	2,961	1951	510,355
1926	4,047	1952	531,719
1927	4,495	1953	839,149
1928	5,529	1954	1,035,282
1929	8,538	1955	165,186
1930	18,319	1956	58,792
1931	8,409	1957	45,640
1932	7,116	1958	45,164
1933	15,875	1959	42,732
1934	8,910	1960	39,750
1935	9,139	1961	39,860
1936	9,534	1962	41,200
1937	9,535	1963	51,230
1938	8,684	1964	41,589
1939	9,376	1965	49,948
1940	8,051	1966	89,638
1941	6,082	1967	107,695
1942	10,603	1968	142,520
1943	16,154	1969	189,572
1944	39,449	1970	265,539
1945	80,760	1971	348,178
1946	116,320	1972	430,213
1947	214,543	1973	655,968
1948	193,852		
1949	289,400		
		Total	7,345,795

Source: Stanley R. Ross, ed., *Views Across the Border: The United States and Mexico* (Albuquerque: University of New Mexico Press, 1978), p. 167.

speakers and on persons with Hispanic surnames, neither group exclusively of Mexican origin. A census estimate in 1978 put "Hispanics" (persons of Hispanic origins, regardless of name) at 12 million, but some people insisted that if all illegal aliens of Hispanic origins were counted that the figure would be 19 million. That would put Hispanics within striking distance of the black minority, because of continuing immigration of Hispanics and because the natural increase of Hispanics was three times that of blacks. In any event, large numbers were involved and it made some people queasy to talk about "control" when the dimensions of the problem were fuzzy.

Not so much law and treaty as economic need propelled and molded the great movement of Mexicans into the United States in recent decades. That is, Mexican laborers and American employers showed scant respect for law, treaty, and regulation. They were encouraged by the feebleness of legislation and enforcement.

Braceros and Wetbacks, 1942–1964

The "temporary" measure for Mexican labor in the United States that went into effect in 1942 lasted until 1964.* That was the *bracero* (arms or labor) program, responding to demands of the farm bloc for ample cheap labor in wartime, when many Americans were in the armed forces.

More than 300,000 agricultural workers, including 219,546 Mexicans, were legally imported between 1943 and 1947 to work in twenty-four states. California got the bulk of the alien workers. Texas was not allowed Mexicans under the agreements because the history of their treatment in that state offended Mexico. Still, Texas received thousands of illegal

---

*See chapter 4 for the original agreement.

Mexican workers, some brought in with the connivance of U.S. officials.

The braceros, supposedly confined to agricultural jobs, willingly worked long, hard hours. They caused employers few social or disciplinary problems because their chief interest was in earning money to improve their lives, preferably in the native village in Mexico. Employers thought their lack of interest in unions to be healthy and possibly even Christian. Finally, Mexicans often would leave the vicinity when their job was done, neither causing police problems nor becoming charges on welfare or charity.

Farmers naturally demanded that the bracero program be extended beyond 1947. Washington was willing to extend; there was more vehement support for it than opposition. The Mexican government was willing, also, though it found it politically expedient not to express this willingness too openly. Bracero remittances helped the balance of payments problem, for Mexico bought more from the United States than it sold there. The program also gave income to Mexicans who, at home, lived at the margin of subsistence. Finally, technical skills some braceros acquired in the U.S. were useful to Mexico.

The braceros affected the population structure of the United States by sometimes hiding in the big, loosely policed society, becoming permanent rather than temporary labor, and by having children. In addition, during those years, some 54,000 Mexicans were granted entry visas to settle in the United States. But the big change in numbers was in the group of illegal entries: wetbacks (*mojados*). The always understaffed INS caught 6,189 in 1943, and the number went up each year, to 182,986 in 1947. The total of 372,902 between 1943 and 1947 no doubt was more than matched by undetected wetbacks.

The illegal migrants found jobs in the United States faster than the U.S. Border Patrol could catch them, while agricultural interests lobbied in Washington for legalization of what was occurring. After negotiations with Mexico, the agreement of 1942 was extended in 1947 to cover the first half of 1948 and that proved to be but the first of many extensions. The maximum number of braceros was reached in 1956, when nearly half a million worked in the United States. The two countries kept making extension agreements, and deploring abuses while doing little about them.

In 1949 the Border Patrol caught 278,538 illegal entrants and 865,318 in 1953. The figures did not show repeaters, some of whom went through the revolving door often enough to be on a first-name basis with the Patrol.

News of the apprehensions put pressure on Washington. The result was Operation Wetback, created in 1954 and conducted by a new commissioner of the INS, retired General Joseph Swing. He coordinated the Border Patrol, state and local officials, and the police. The declared target was all illegal aliens, but operations concentrated on Mexicans, sweeping through Mexican-American barrios in southwestern cities. Some frightened Mexicans fled south across the border. In 1954 the agents found 1.075 million illegal aliens.

Some Mexicans illegally living in the United States were deported together with their American-born children, who were citizens! The agents increased their practice of stopping individuals on the streets if they thought they looked "Mexican," asking identification. That was infuriating for citizens of Mexican-American origin, and some resisted the officers. Although the INS claimed that it now had the illegal alien problem under control, the public was not impressed. Critics in both the United States and Mexico complained of "police-state" methods, and Operation Wetback was abandoned. Apprehension of aliens was down to 252,605 in 1955.

But the bracero program went on. So did wetback movement, nicely helped by the continued refusal of Congress to punish employers for hiring aliens illegally in the country. The general Immigration and Nationality Act of 1952 had "dealt with" the Mexican question by declaring it against the law to help aliens enter or remain illegally, yet it failed to specify that hiring such illegal aliens was improper! It was the old story of vigorous special interest groups impressing congressmen more than their poorly organized and only tepidly concerned critics.

Criticism of the bracero program did increase. The civil rights movement contributed by focusing on the treatment both of illegal aliens and of Mexican-Americans generally. The Chicano movement developed objections to the bracero program. Intellectual and church groups chimed in. Some business groups favored an end to the bracero connection. Some people claimed that bracero laborers recruited people from their Mexican villages to enter as wetbacks. So the program was abandoned in 1964. Some small-scale contract labor was permitted, however, from time to time thereafter.

Changes in immigration law in 1965 and 1968 put the Western Hemisphere into a revised quota system, with a limit of 120,000. A new law, effective January 1, 1977, retained the total of 120,000 for the Western Hemisphere, with the Mexican share set at 20,000 per year.

The arguments in recent years over admittance of Mexicans were rendered somewhat dubious by the fact that cheap labor was provided beyond the national quotas by admitting refugees, usually to escape war, revolution, and political or religious persecution. This was in accordance with American tradition, but it also served employers who wanted cheap labor. There were such acts to admit refugees in 1945, 1948, 1950, and 1953. An act of 1959 to admit refugees from Castro's Cuba resulted ultimately in admission of some 600,000. And in the 1970s refugees were admitted from Vietnam. The U.S. attorney general was given discretionary authority to grant (in consultation with Congress) immigration rights to refugees. In June 1978 he authorized issuance to 12,000 East Europeans (mostly Soviet Jews) and 25,000 Indochinese; in December 1978 another 21,875 Indochinese; and in early 1979 some

60,000 more Soviet and Indochinese refugees. The policy was a matter of some dispute, but there were both liberal and conservative groups that wanted to continue it, in some form, for different reasons.

As the new Western Hemisphere law went into effect in January 1977, there were some 300,000 visa applications on file for Western Hemisphere countries and 60 percent of them were for Mexicans. Restrictive legislation obviously had its largest impact on Mexico, but the real result was not restriction of Mexican immigration but its continuation on an illegal basis.

"Chickens" and the Border Patrol

The immigration tide was set in motion in Mexico mostly by word of mouth. Returning braceros and wetbacks said the patrols were not too serious, *entonces vale la pena* ("thus, it is worth the trouble"). Furthermore, they said, a man living in the U.S. for only one year could, with luck, save more than someone could save in a lifetime in Mexico—even $1,000 or $2,000. Although not all migrants were lucky or provident, the appeal of America was as great today as it was for Irish and German immigrants a century earlier. Americans scarcely realized that the Mexican migrants were moved by that holy "American" thing, the lust for opportunity. Nor did they realize that nowhere in the world was there so great a disparity between the average incomes of the populations of neighboring countries.

Returnees to the Mexican villages mostly spoke well of the U.S. In this they were unlike critics within the permanent Mexican-American community. And the more rabid Mexican and American critics of United States society simply believed that the villagers could only view their experience north of the border with disgust.

Remittances of money by workers in the States spoke nearly as loudly in Mexico as the tales of returnees. Some villages had a tradition of decades of labor across the border and were periodically half-emptied of working-age men.

Migrants generally went from their villages to the border area and either tried their luck alone, or found help. Border towns burst their seams with people waiting to cross into the visible promised land. It was easy to locate, or be located by, a "coyote"—an agent who directed the would-be migrant "chicken" ("pallo") to a "chicken handler" ("pollero"), who took him or her across the border.*

Prices for the trip into the United States long ran from $200 to $400 a head, but in the later 1970s rose as high as $600, partly due to general price inflation. It also was due to improved surveillance in some areas, including the use of searchlights during the critical hours of darkness and helicopters in daytime to ferret out those who made it across. Although the price might be high, it was possible to borrow money for a crossing or to use a more cut-rate, inefficient, and dangerous *pollero.*

The smugglers generally led their "chickens" across a rough and poorly patrolled place on the border at night, to trucks hidden on side roads. The problem then was to quickly hide the chickens in a city barrio or with a conniving farmer. Sometimes smugglers sold false U.S. documents to the migrants.

Some poor "chickens" were killed by the smugglers out of greed or fright. Some died of suffocation in car trunks, or succumbed in closed trucks used to obscure the ravages of hunger, thirst, overcrowding—the ancient weaknesses of a poor population. Still, illegal entry continued to appeal to indigent Mexicans. Of course, it was the only chance they had.

Long standing complaints about the INS were emphasized in January 1980 by a series of newspaper articles in the *New York Times* on "The Tarnished Door." Many types of misdeeds were spelled out, committed not only by INS personnel but by lawyers and others who sell services, sometimes worth-

---

*Smugglers of people also were called *pasadores* and *enganchadores.*

less, to foreigners wishing to enter or legalize their status in the United States.

While these massive and sometimes ugly events were occurring, many Americans continued to believe that such phenomena only existed in places like Bangladesh and Viet Nam.

During all this, the border watch in the United States remained feeble, as it had been since the Treaty of Guadalupe Hidalgo of 1848. In 1964, with legal crossings in the tens of millions, and under various rules there were 1,790 immigration personnel on the border. In May 1973, the load of legal crossings having greatly increased and the number of wetbacks at a high level, immigration personnel totaled a mere 2,155.

Although there were periodic probes of alleged corruption among immigration personnel, little was found. The problem was that generally the American government, reflecting public opinion, did not much care. There was little public pressure for stronger laws. Budgets for patrol and safeguard measures were small. The border was a sieve and a joke. It was known that some Mexicans illegally residing in the United States went to Mexico for the holidays, knowing they could return north much as they pleased.

The Border Patrol was generally not popular in the border area because it interfered with an illegal labor system that workers and employers generally supported. The Patrol was accused of harshness and suffered the common lower-class fear and distaste for "cops."

INS personnel along the Mexican border have achieved among Mexicans an evil reputation for brutality, corruption, and the sexual abuse of women. But some groups approved of the patrol, at times—for example, labor organizers when wetbacks served commercial farmers as strike-breakers. Still, INS personnel claimed they were not properly supported. When an injunction in 1973 in Los Angeles stopped an INS roundup of illegal aliens, an angry INS employee said that the

United States should either get tough or admit it wanted Mexicans as "slave labor."

Rise of American Fears

The question of illegal aliens—especially from Mexico—caused more unease as the estimated numbers mounted. Then in the mid-1970s economic recessions in Mexico and the United States heightened fears—in the United States of immigration, in Mexico of harsh U.S. measures to cut it down. Bad U.S. relations with Mexico in the later years of the term (1970–76) of President Echeverría made discussion of any matters difficult. He had made himself a spokesman for the Third World and was vociferously critical of the United States. President José López Portillo (inaugurated December 1976) wanted better relations but could not afford to appear to surrender to the United States, especially on immigration or the petroleum issue.

In the 1970s an increased stridence entered discussions in government, the media, and intellectual and reform groups. Gigantic statistics floated about like bogeymen, altering their shapes to suit the fancies of partisans. Some voices were raised to turn back the "invasion" from Mexico. One writer said the country was "chaotically polyglot."

In 1976 and 1977 some Americans mounted an anti-alien crusade, partly as a backlash against domestic economic, political, and social conditions that they could not control. It was a time of disenchantment with government due to high taxes, recollections of the Vietnam War and Watergate, and the continuing observation of government troubles in New York City and Cleveland. It always was easy to blame foreigners for problems.

The debate was not stilled by the news in 1976 and thereafter of the great new oil discoveries in Mexico. Although there was hope that these discoveries would give relief from the OPEC oil cartel, there was little public awareness that concessions to Mexico on immigration and other issues might be the price.

The debate in the U.S. and in Mexico reached new peaks of emotion after President Carter on August 4, 1977, delivered to Congress proposals for a new immigration law. He called for full amnesty for aliens who had been in the country at least seven years, giving them permanent resident status and allowing them to bring their families to the United States. That certainly would reduce the number of illegal aliens, but its other effects might be equally important.

Carter also proposed that aliens living here illegally before January 1, 1977, but for less than seven years, be permitted to remain and allowed to work. They could not, however, bring their families or receive most social services. Whether this would be a contribution to either immigration control or to justice was not clear.

Carter certainly sounded willing to try to make future control stricter. He asked for 260 more INS inspectors to detect aliens working illegally. He also proposed two thousand more enforcement officers on the border. Those would be steps in the direction of better control, although the numbers seemed inadequate.

The most courageous, and potentially effective, measure Carter proposed was penalties for employers of illegal aliens: fines of $1,000 per alien working illegally and criminal penalties for employers repeatedly violating the law. Carter also suggested a more forge-proof Social Security card as a prerequisite for employment. Such measures suggested in the past had failed in Congress, one identification of tepid public support for control of illegal immigration.

Carter's proposal brought on a storm of criticism. It was immoral to legalize illegal activity by granting the amnesties. Such a program would encourage more illegal immigration from Mexico. It would lead to more forging of rent receipts, Social Security documents, and other papers to prove past residence in the United States. It was claimed that 50 million Mexicans would eventually come because amnestied aliens could bring in their families. The Ku Klux Klan threatened violence to preserve a "white man's country."

The *New York Times* (August 8, 1977), editorializing under the title "Sweeping Back the Illegal Tide," began by finding the Carter proposals a "creditable" effort and ended by finding them sadly defective. It deplored "solutions" that concentrated on the largely agricultural areas of the Southwest. Amnesties might make city problems worse by increasing the demand for social services to serve the entering families of fully amnestied aliens, about a third of which cost would come from city and state funds. It might be even worse in the case of the partially amnestied, because they were ineligible for Medicaid, food stamps, or welfare but would have to be looked after, possibly at local expense.

Debate of the 1970s

The debate was both economic and political or "spiritual." Of course, in both countries the two categories overlapped and interacted. Reasonable people favored an agreement helpful to both countries. But they knew that it had to *appear* helpful to simple and sometimes passionate citizens in Mexico and the United States. That might not be easy to arrange. Possibly, political factors—often emotion-laden—would long postpone a reasonable economic settlement that included a "solution" to the migration problem.

Many points of view flourished on both sides of the border. In the U.S., clashes of opinion on all subjects were so uproarious and incessant that foreigners long had wondered how the republic endured. And in Mexico, for all the semidictatorship of one party, much discussion was allowed within and without party and government. The lush variety in both countries of plausible and exotic opinion, often flowering into incidents of declamation, defamation, march and countermarch, and petition and prayer seemed limited only by the passion, knowledge, political ambition, and intellectual and moral zeal of the participants. It made politicians—mostly a phlegmatic lot— uneasy.

Economic Arguments

Many economic, semieconomic, pseudoeconomic claims were made. Some were poorly based on data; some were sheer fantasy.

The basic Mexican view was that the key to migration was the state of the economy in Mexico. Mexicans would stay home if there were decent jobs for them. Thus, all economic arguments were peripheral to the need for economic development in Mexico. If the United States wanted fewer Mexican migrants, it would have to help develop the Mexican economy. That Mexican opinion became stronger in the 1970s. President López Portillo late in the decade reiterated the view that Mexico wanted to export goods rather than men. He declared that more trade with, and more investment from, the United States would benefit both countries, including private enterprise.

That was a rational position for Mexico to take and probably the best "answer" to the problem of illegal migration. It was, however, a potentially risky and expensive prescription that the United States resisted taking. Who could measure the cost? A few Americans said that admitting Mexican labor was the cheapest form of aid and that no more should be offered. Some Americans did not even want to offer that.

An issue that long had troubled Americans was that illegal Mexican aliens deprived U.S. citizens of jobs. That plausible fear was not reduced by the absence of much evidence to support it. There were not enough data on illegal aliens in jobs, or whether they displaced citizens; but there was much evidence of Americans refusing the sort of tasks that illegal aliens did. Responses to job ads in New York City, for example, showed that, and in 1977 a Virginia apple grower claimed he hired U.S. hands to pick fruit but that they left during the first day because the work was too hard. Probably it was partly because of low wages. No doubt citizens would take some of those jobs at higher wages. But how much higher? And how many of them would pick lettuce or wash dishes at any wage?

It was argued that stiff control of U.S. employers would solve the problem. But would public opinion support the cost of enforcement? And would employers then move to foreign countries to find cheap labor?

Some people simply argued that with 6 million Americans unemployed and with 6 million Mexicans illegally here, just oust the latter and employ the former. As far back as 1959 the *New York Times* portrayed an Alice-in-the-Wonderland-of-the-Southwest, wondering how Mexican farm hands could be imported on the grounds of a "labor shortage," when 5 million Americans were unemployed. The Red Queen retorted that Alice did not understand the American agricultural system. Neither did many Americans.

In April 1979 a *New York Times* editorial said the city had between .5 million and 1.5 million illegal aliens and that small businesses "relished" the cheap labor, while City Hall deplored the cost of providing the aliens with services. The paper found that the cheap labor kept marginal enterprises in operation but probably deprived some citizens of jobs. It thought "rooting out" aliens might be prohibitively expensive, but that amnesty for them had "drawbacks." As this mish-mash suggests, they decided that there was "no perfect answer" to the problem. That, the *Times* intoned, permitted "forgiveness" of the federal government's slowness to act, but it was "inexcusable" that it did not aid states and cities "saddled with illegals." If anything could be made of this whirlpool, it was that taxpayers in general should pay for the insistence of certain localities on using large numbers of illegal alien workers. A year later, the *New York Times* editorialized in an especially graphic fashion that the United States has a clear immigration policy: "The Wink." It has restrictive legislation, and deliberately winks at massive violations. Cheap labor is wanted by many American citizens.

The low wages of illegal aliens caused hot complaint and some debate because the statistics were imperfect. An INS survey in 1975 found that two-thirds of the illegal workers interviewed made less than $2.50 an hour, while only 5 percent made more than $4.50 an hour, then the average hourly wage of U.S. workers. Critics said it was a small · ·ple and that in any event even at $2.50 an hour Mexicans would be middle class in their own country, even though they fell below the poverty line in the United States.

Labor spokespeople, on the other hand, said that such wages were so low that they forced American citizens to use welfare, unwilling to accept such a low standard of living. Some legal Mexicans and Mexican-Americans in the U.S. echoed that argument, being among those most damaged by illegal alien labor.

A Mexican scholar in 1977 said that Mexicans seldom made much in the United States. It was partly because they did not stay long—85 percent less than a year, and only 2.7 percent longer than 16 months. He claimed it also was due to the fact that expenses were much higher in the United States. Other investigators found that Mexicans spent little in this country. The Mexican further argued that a Mexican rarely made more than $800 during his stay in the United States. That figure certainly was low, even though many illegal Mexican aliens suffered income tax and Social Security deductions and their language difficulty and fear of arrest made it relatively easy for them to be cheated by employers, stores, banks, and money lenders.

Social service costs for illegal Mexican workers also sparked debate. There was wide belief in the United States that they constituted a huge charge on the public, forcing up taxes. One report put the charge at $13 billion a year for the education and welfare of aliens. One reason California voters in 1977 and 1978 demanded controls on property taxes was their belief that Mexican aliens received services they did not pay for. In 1976 the INS estimated that there were more than 8 million foreigners illegally living in the U.S. and that they were being subsidized to the amount of $200 million. That guess was at least much less than the frequent vague claims of "enormous" costs.

Serious studies, in fact, indicated that probably no huge charge occurred. Illegal aliens seldom used social services, especially in the Southwest, where Mexicans were most numerous. Many illegals are not in United States long enough to qualify for benefits. Many illegal Mexican aliens were afraid to apply for Social Security benefits or welfare lest their illegal status be detected. Some were unfamiliar with such systems. Many were diffident about using English or anything that brought them in touch with officialdom.

The fact was that by federal, and often state, law illegal aliens were ineligible for Social Security, food stamps, and unemployment insurance. The sample studies that were made nearly all showed that few illegal Mexicans got social services. Even more, there was reason to believe that they paid in more than they got back, and thus subsidized the social services of others.

Usage of social services may change, however. Suits are being brought before federal courts in Texas to compel the public schools to accept the children of illegal aliens without special tuition fees. Recent rulings by the U.S. Supreme Court and the federal Justice Department support these demands.

On the other hand, whatever the aliens thought about services, they could not avoid paying income and Social Security taxes, because they were withheld from their wages. Nor could they escape sales taxes. That made unsurprising the finding of a sample study in 1976 that 77 percent of illegals paid Social Security taxes and 73 percent paid federal income tax, but that only 4 percent had children in school, and one half of one percent received welfare. The young and predominantly male illegal aliens would receive little from the major types of social service since they did not qualify for old age assistance, disability payments, being female heads of households, or dependent, poor children.

Mexican alien wages remitted to Mexico irritated some Americans who were weak in economics but knew what they disliked. It seemed likely that by the late 1950s such remittances were possibly $100 million a year and comprised Mexico's third largest source of foreign exchange. By the 1970s remittances were often stated at well over $200 million annually. Mexican nationalists disputed the estimates as too high. In any event, there was all-too-little discussion of whether or not this represented "loss" to the United States, or a bargain price for useful labor.

The economic argument over Mexican immigrants (legal or illegal) seldom was attacked in toto. One problem was that the data were poor, so that it was difficult to know how much the cheap labor lowered prices. It was also hard to set that off against welfare costs for legal labor that was driven (if it was) into unemployment. The largest deficiency in the discussion was, perhaps, the unwillingness to admit that the highly educated American population resisted taking menial jobs. Thus, the country "needed"—certainly insisted on—immigrants to wash dishes, shine shoes, and pick lettuce. Although there was some recognition of that, it was not a subject that was likely to become popular.

A major Mexican argument was that if many of its migrant citizens were dumped back across the border there would be massive social disorders and an economic collapse, which would affect the United States. Some Mexican employers also thought, erroneously, that their payroll was raised by emigration. Americans who said that an effective border control would be too costly did not bother to balance cost against benefits. In the late 1970s some demographic groups in the United States developed the line that big illegal immigration might cancel the benefits of declining fertility and zero population growth. Their simplistic arguments for the economic benefits of such zero growth were not convincing. Neither was much of the rest of the debate on the economic effects of illegal alien labor.

Political/Spiritual Arguments

The immigration issue stimulated statements directed to political, emotional, even spiritual, needs or problems. Some were vague, others vituperative. A Mexican in May 1977, objecting to Carter's plans on immigration, said the president was "myopic" and making "unilateral decisions on our economy." In August 1977 the U.S. secretary of labor told the *New York Times* that while illegal aliens worked cheaply, their children might agitate for better living conditions and become the "civil rights problem of the 1980s." One wondered whether he objected equally to better living conditions and to civil rights.

Much comment was nationalistic or xenophobic or both. There were objections by Mexicans when their border officials increased cooperation with their U.S. counterparts. Mexicans sometimes claimed that dependence on the earnings of migrants promoted economic dependence on the United States. Statements as innocent of economic knowledge as that could only be labeled "political." Mexicans objected to Mexican performance of "demeaning" jobs in the United States as being a violation of Mexican "dignity." The implication that being unemployed in Mexico was more dignified was sheer romantic nationalism. There was Mexican objection to migration to live amid U.S. racial and cultural discrimination. It was said that there was no welcome wagon (as used in middle class districts of the United States) for Mexicans. That was true.

United States nationalism on the issue often was warm, too, with a revival of nativist emotion. There were fears of "cultural degeneration" and racial mixture. Were Mexicans assimilable? Vague flapdoodle said aliens sapped the national strength. Why didn't Mexican migrants learn English as earlier stocks did? Much of it was like the litany recited against immigrants in the 1840s and '50s and after World War I.

There also were Mexican objections to migration as contaminating. The immoral life of the United States would corrupt Mexicans. Good Catholics would become Protestants. (In fact, neither outcome was widely observed among Mexican-Americans.) It was claimed that the absence of the father when he went north disrupted family life. That rather underplayed the family deprivations of ordinary Mexican village life. A few Mexicans complained that returned migrants were "restless"—that is, harder to control.

George Meany, former chief of the AFL-CIO, in 1977 accused a senator of trying to reestablish a bracero program for his own personal gain. That was a sample of the heat the issue aroused. Even in the absence of a new bracero program, what existed promoted frequent rows. If a farmer tried "properly" and failed to find U.S. citizens to work his fields, the Labor Department could certify the use of foreigners. With that, the INS could issue visas for temporary work. Such action, following suggested approval by President Carter, brought 809 Mexicans in 1977 to work farms near Presidio, Texas. Protests came at once from the Labor Department and organized labor, with claims that American workers were available and doubts that the farmers would treat the Mexicans properly.

Law Enforcement Agencies and Mexican-Americans

So how to stop illegal immigration? The obvious methods were not to let people in or to deny them jobs. The latter meant penalizing employers who used aliens illegally in the country. For years, that met effective opposition. Bills introduced to that end failed in the Congress in 1973. President Carter's proposal in 1977 to punish employers on those lines did find some support from labor unions. And late in the year, public opinion polls showed that a majority of the population favored such a measure. When and if that could be translated into a congressional majority was not certain.

A national identity card, it long had been realized, would be useful for alien control, including application for jobs. But the idea always met the charge that identity cards were un-American and a step toward a police state. There were, however, some congressmen in the 1970s who favored the idea. Opponents claimed it would be difficult to make forge-proof cards yet were not interested to know that France and Germany managed to do so. They pointed, rather, at such indications as the seizure in Los Angeles in 1973 of 60,000 counterfeit alien registration cards of high quality.

In 1977 a cabinet committee refused to approve the idea of forge-proof Social Security cards for national identity purposes. They claimed it would be expensive, at an estimated $500 million, and that it might violate the civil liberties of both aliens and citizens. President Carter did endorse the idea of such cards in 1977, but there were no signs that Congress soon would agree with him. Nevertheless, the possibility of such cards being used seemed greater than a few years earlier.

Some other control measures were suggested, and sometimes tried, that apparently would get little support as panaceas:

1. Reliance on roundups to locate aliens illegally in the country was unlikely because they had a bad press, often with good reason. That was the case in November 1976 when an ill-advised search at a soccer game in Washington, D.C., led to panic as people fled, some even jumping into the Tidal Basin. That was an unedifying sight in front of the statue of Thomas Jefferson.

2. In the late 1970s a vigilante group in Southern California tried to "aid" in keeping out Mexicans. But the appeal of vigilante methods seemed to be confined to a lunatic fringe.

3. It was suggested that the Constitution be amended to discourage pregnant foreign women from slipping across the

border to have their children, which qualified the mother for permanent residence in the U.S. One "reform" suggestion was that only when both parents were U.S. citizens would a child receive citizenship at birth. Such ideas raised no enthusiasm.

4. There were suggestions (all unofficial) that the problem would be eased if Mexico slowed its population growth. The number of enemies that notion could boast was so obvious that it never rose above a murmur.

Firmer physical controls at the border always had some support. Congress had a long record, however, of resisting the idea of a really large number of border guards. It did permit a bit of fencing, searchlights, radar, infrared scopes, electronic ground sensors, dogs, and dragstrips that airplanes overflew in the morning to spy the tracks of passers in the night. Those things were never used enough to affect total illegal entry.

Furthermore, many actual or suggested increases of physical control measures brought objections from Mexico that it was being singled out for insulting and sometimes inhuman attentions. Sometimes such complaints in Mexico aroused considerable nationalist clamor. Thus, a Mexico City leftist magazine in February 1978 thought it worthwhile to say that the United States used on-the-border detection devices tried out in Vietnam, and efficient arms for "the hunting of man."

There also were increasing objections from civil libertarians in the United States to many of the methods tried or suggested for controlling illegal immigration from Mexico. The American Civil Liberties Union in 1973 obtained an injunction to stop INS raids on Mexican-American-area hotels, apartment buildings, and places of work, seizing aliens and sending them to the border for deportation. The ACLU charged that among the deportees were United States citizens. Objections to that sort of axe-work by public officials went back to the 1930s and earlier. But now the civil rights movement was stronger than ever before.

A related incident in 1977 further indicated that government could not safely resort to bludgeon methods. A court action brought government admission that it had improperly subtracted from regular Western Hemisphere immigration quotas the 145,000 Cuban refugees it gave priority for entry between 1969 and 1971. They should have been admitted under the special legislation existing for Cuban refugees, and another 145,000 admitted from other countries of the Western Hemisphere should have been admitted. Appointed officials had, in effect, rewritten the immigration law. The "error" was what civil libertarians considered an all-too-typical arbitrary decision by bureaucrats—in this case, those in the State Department and INS.

All this helped explain the violent opposition to fences and walls for the border. An INS announcement in 1977 that the twenty-seven miles of fence in the San Diego and El Paso areas would be extended six miles led to cries by nationalists in Mexico that the fence would run from coast to coast. It touched off rumors—that is, inventions—that the U.S. Air Force would be used against migrants. Predictably, Mexicans also said it constituted U.S. pressure to get Mexican oil cheaply, thus was "diplomatic blackmail." Newspapers talked about the "tortilla curtain" and a "Berlin Wall."

Any fence extension was likely to cause some grumbling, but the proposal of 1977 included sharp metal spikes at the top that were denounced as cruel. The INS, retreating from this, did not abandon foolishness completely but substituted barbed wire. It later fell from that position in the face of more blasts of criticism. A congressman called the original fence proposal "bigoted" and "insane." Stupid," "inept," and "insensitive" would have been more accurate.

Even existing fences often don't help. The border section between San Diego and Tijuana continues to be the target for the most massive and uncontrolled movement from Mexico to the United States. INS personnel there call it the "combat zone." The irresistible pressure of poor Mexicans wanting to enter the rich labor market of California simply flattens chain link fences that pretend to interfere.

Over the years there were suggestions for a huge wall along the entire border, possibly patrolled by the army, with orders to shoot illegal entrants. There was little support for such drastic measures.

All this reflected the obvious fact that the United States could very severely restrict crossings of the Mexican border if it took strong physical measures. But Americans were not ready for a wall. Would some future crisis make a wall popular?

At the least, it could be hoped that Americans would realize that there was no cheap or easy answer to the problem of illegal immigration from Mexico.

A wall, alas, not only would poison relations with Mexico but it might merely shift the problem of illegal entry from the Mexican border to other areas. Mexicans would still come in some numbers, by sea and air, over and around the wall. More importantly, perhaps, immigrants would come in increasing numbers from other countries.

For some years it had been clear that the large majority of illegal aliens apprehended in the United States were Mexican, mostly caught in the Southwest. Surveillance in the cities of the East was less effective. The question was: Could it be made much more effective in urban areas at an affordable price and with methods the American public would support?

A 1976 government report showed that most illegal aliens came from fifteen countries: Mexico, Dominican Republic, Haiti, Jamaica, Guatemala, Colombia, Peru, Ecuador, the Philippines, Korea, Thailand, Greece, India, Iran, and Nigeria. The pressures to emigrate from those poor countries would not soon disappear.

As with the illegal importing of drugs, if Americans did not want to stop using illegal alien labor, a wall of brass enclosing the entire country would not keep out needy workers.*

There was a final irony. Many Americans thought that

---

*See chapters 8 and 9 for more comment on the problem of illegal Mexicans in the United States.

Mexicans lusted for the good life in "God's Country." They imagined the migrants wanted to stay and would be forever an unassimilable lump in the society.

Not so. The evidence indicated that most of the illegal entrants from Mexico preferred to remain only temporarily in the United States. It seemed likely that if Mexico were prosperous, few Mexicans would settle in the States, or even work there temporarily.

On the other hand, it appeared that most non-Mexican illegal aliens preferred to remain in the United States, mostly in cities. Official and private surveys supported that conclusion. Thus, although Mexican laborers often spoke well of the United States, they thought of it as a good place to visit; but they did not want to live there. They did not want to become "Chicanos."

SEVEN

Mexican-Americans and Chicanos

Will the Mexican-American community eventually be much like those of Irish, German, Polish, and Italian nationalities? That is, largely assimilated and little interested in the old homeland, or very important to the latter? No one knows; but assimilation has certainly proceeded more slowly for Mexicans than for Europeans. Mexican immigrants have met more prejudice and discrimination and have been slower to adopt English. Unlike other immigrant groups, the Mexican-American still receives large additions from the homeland, thus slowing assimilation. It is probable that the Chicano movement that began in the 1960s speeded assimilation, despite assertions that bilingualism and cultural distinctiveness were non-negotiable aims. Most likely, the next-door position of Mexico will not bolster "chicanismo" unless other Americans refuse to admit Mexican-Americans to full equality. The Chicano movement helped make Mexican-Americans more assertive politically. How many more Mexican-American citizens will be assimilated to the melting pot is as much a matter for speculation as the idea that Chicanos can serve the U.S. as a "bridge" with Mexico or with all of Spanish America.

Rejection and Assimilation

Rejection of Mexicans and Mexican-Americans has long
been the predominant attitude of an Anglo community that
wanted cheap maids, railway workers, lettuce choppers, and
busboys of Mexican heritage rather than friends and fellow
citizens. "Greasers" have met more prejudice and discrimination than "hunkies," "squareheads," and "wops."

Mexicans have met not only the old English-American
prejudice against Latins in general and Spaniards in particular, but also disdainful attitudes toward Indians and toward
"racial mixtures." Such attitudes are uninhibited by an embarrassing lack of knowledge about the qualities of Latins or
Indians, or the nature of race, or the effects of racial mixture.
Prejudice, of course, also grew out of jealousy and fear of
economic, social, and political competition.

Mexican-Americans have confronted prejudice and discrimination in bars, hotels, cafes, barbershops, swimming
pools, trains, courts of justice, real estate offices, and on a
thousand other obnoxious occasions. The darker the skin of
the Mexican-American, the more likely he or she is treated
as an inferior creature. One of the authors of this book remembers as a boy in Banning, California, the special section
of the little cinema designated for "Mexes."

Mexico's consuls in the Southwest have often protested discrimination against Mexican-Americans, one source of ani-
mosity between the two countries. It was especially infuriating
that while many Mexican-Americans fought valiantly in World
War II, the Sleepy Lagoon case in Los Angeles revealed the
ugly depths of Anglo prejudice. Seventeen Mexican-American
youths were convicted, on circumstantial evidence, of beating
to death a young Mexican-American. The press declared the
"innate" depravity of the Mexican-American character, but a
higher court later found the youths innocent. Anglo servicemen
provoked the notorious "pachuco" or "Zoot Suit" race riots by
attacking Mexican-Americans while the police looked the other

way, and the press applauded. Another nasty instance of prejudice came to national attention in 1948 when the body of Felix Longoria, killed in battle in the Philippines, was returned to Texas for burial. The only mortician in Longoria's hometown would not let his chapel be used. It was only marginally comforting that a national outcry led to Longoria's burial in Arlington National Cemetery.

Americans outside the Southwest have been much more familiar with prejudice against blacks than against browns. The systematic humiliation of Mexican-Americans came to general attention, however, when the novel *Giant* was made into a movie in 1956 and handsome Rock Hudson was sneered at by Anglo Texans as the offspring of Mexican-Americans. The fact that he became a physician presumably reflected discredit on the medical profession.

There is an old argument as to whether race or culture or both comprise "Mexican-Americanness." The Bureau of the Census solved its part of the problem in 1950 by turning to the use of the classification, "white persons with Spanish surnames." That put Mexican-Americans into the larger group of Hispanics and eliminated any official question of race. Some spokesmen of the Chicano movement, however, have insisted that Indian race and culture were essential components of "chicanismo"; yet some Mexican-Americans ignore their Indian heritage, strongly preferring to be known as Latinos, Mexican-Americans, Spaniards, or Hispanos.

Estimates of the number of people in the United States of Mexican origin generally run between six and seven million, although pro-Mexican-American parties claim up to fifteen million. Mexican-American families have more children than the national average, but the differential has declined in the 1960s and 1970s. The bulk of the Mexican-American population in the late 1970s has remained in Arizona, California, Colorado, New Mexico, and Texas, although a tendency to move outward has persisted. Mexican-Americans, originally a rural people, joined the rest of the American population in moving to town, and by the late 1960s were nearly 80 percent urban. In some urban and rural areas of the Southwest, Mexican-Americans outnumber Anglos—as Chicano publicists became fond of pointing out.

The despised Mexican-Americans have endured, as have the "Paddies" of the "No Irish Need Apply" era, the poor Jews from eastern Europe, illiterate peasants from Sicily, and the "Pollocks" of Upton Sinclair's *The Jungle*. They have been a "disadvantaged" group; society has obstructed the development of their talents and their access to opportunities for advancement. The natural result has been the alienation of many Mexican-Americans from Anglo society. A poor social and economic situation generally has made escape from the ghetto difficult and created bitterness.

Some Mexican-Americans have moved easily into the general society, and many youngsters born in the United States retain only shreds of the old speech and culture. But recognition of partial assimilation has been obscured by imprecise statistics and by the emotionalism of the Chicano movement. Many Chicano leaders object to Anglo insistence on assimilation into the dominant and supposedly superior culture. Some Anglos claim that Mexican-Americans are fundamentally less assimilable than other immigrant groups, while highly respected Anglo scholars say that the evidence does not support such a notion. But evidence is irrelevant to bigotry towards inferior "races" or enthusiasm for resisting the "cultural imperialism" of Anglos.

The Chicano Movement—La Raza

The Chicano movement that began in the mid-1960s has its roots in a million slights, and in a conviction that fair treatment depends on an end to docility. This new self-assertiveness has rested on an accumulation of statistics on the disadvantaged status of the Mexican-American at work, school, in segregated housing, and in unfair—sometimes brutal—

treatment by public authorities. It has been aided by the movement of Mexican-Americans to cities, where discussion and organization are easier there than in migrant labor camps or isolated farms. It received impetus after World War II from the assertiveness of Mexican-American veterans who had a splendid combat record. In the 1960s and 1970s militant Chicanos said, "Count our Congressional Medals of Honor!"

The civil rights movement of the 1950s and thereafter also stimulated Mexican-American action, following court decisions against school segregation and unfair electoral practices. In addition, the big new antipoverty programs pointed to an enlarged public receptivity to correction of past abuses. Finally, improvement in the conditions of life of some Mexican-Americans contributed to outrage at the continuing excess of prejudice and discrimination.

Chicano leaders and groups are diverse and disagree on aims and tactics. There are major concentrations of interest on cultural and spiritual matters, labor problems, and on political participation. Leaders agree in condemning the exploitation of Mexican-Americans and that a spirit of chicanismo can somehow be used to help end it. Yet there is much disagreement as to the content of chicanismo, or even as to the use of that term of obscure origins that conservative Mexican-Americans often dislike. Some Mexican-Americans have wanted to work within the system, as Congressman Henry González, who in April 1969 attacked Chicano militants and what he called their program of hate. Militant Chicanos have, in turn, called men like the congressman "coconuts"—brown outside, white inside. Some even adopt the black epithet "Uncle Tom," inveighing against the collaborating "Tío Tomás."

There has been much disagreement within and without the Chicano movement as to how to aid Mexican-Americans. When President Lyndon Johnson in June 1967 created the Inter-Agency Committee on Mexican-American Affairs, it at once fell into disorder over how to proceed.

Despite these disagreements, there is no question but that several dynamic leaders have been important to the explosive birth of the movement. César Chávez, leader of poor migrant farm workers, provided the initial spark. Born in California not far from the Mexican border in 1928, he shared with his parents the life of migrant laborers during the Great Depression that followed. He was fortunate to achieve even eighth-grade schooling. In the later 1950s and early 1960s he overcame with great difficulty some of the apathy and suspicion of the migrant workers and slowly enrolled some in his United Farm Workers (UFW). Chávez in 1965 issued the "Delano Proclamation," calling for a "social movement" and justice, with which "we will overcome!" He achieved national reknown in 1965 with strikes of workers on California vineyards and rose plantations. "Viva La Huega"—Hurrah for the Strike!—chanted the strikers, and college students echoed them.

Chávez' appeal rested on his courageous personality, on the justice of the cause of the underpaid and badly treated workers, on the civil rights enthusiasm of the time. He seemed to many observers—and he achieved much more coverage in the media—a good and dedicated man, opposed to violence, industrious, personally abstemious, apparently not ambitious for himself, a man of strong religious feeling, willing to fast to publicize the needs of the workers. His cause and his personality appealed powerfully to militant or idealistic university students. A workers' song of the time prayed "long live Chávez and the Virgin who guides him."

Reies López Tijerina became a folk hero to poor Mexican-American villagers and farmers in New Mexico, an inspiration to the Chicano movement, and a bogeyman to the Anglo establishment. He claims that much of the land of New Mexico belonged to the villagers, some of whose ancestors had lived in the area long before the Spaniards came.

López Tijerina, born in 1927, like Chávez is the son of migrant farm workers and received little schooling. While still in his teens he became a preacher in the fundamentalist Assembly of God Church. In 1962 he founded the Alianza Federal de Mercedes (land grants) to "recover" the lands of the villagers. This later became the Alianza Federal de los Pueblos Libres (Federal Alliance of Free Towns), which proclaimed its right to self-government and a separate "nationalism." López Tijerina and his people "arrested" some Forest Rangers (supposedly trespassing on village lands) in 1965 and in 1967 engaged in a gun battle in the process of trying to arrest a district attorney. For Chicanos "El Tigre"—The Tiger—was born. Some Anglos thought that bloody revolution—possibly inspired by Fidel Castro—impended. La Causa of López Tijerina was a fiery call to action, and that was what the Chicano movement wanted.

Rodolfo "Corky" González is a city boy (Denver) who showed that he could make it as a boxer, businessman, and Democratic party politician. He was the coordinator of the "Viva Kennedy" campaign in Colorado in 1960. Then he decided that the Democratic programs for the disadvantaged were merely cosmetic, so he withdrew from mainstream politics, founding in 1965 La Cruzada Para Justicia (The Crusade for Justice). It did useful work in such fields as education and legal aid. He advocated Chicano "nationalism" to help "liberation," by "revolutionary" means, stating that Anglos only respected power. He spoke of the "communalism" of Chicanos and glorified La Raza. He also advocated "machismo" (courage and daring) in pursuing aims, one of which was the "Spiritual Plan of Aztlán," to revive the ancient spirit of the Aztecs. The five-day Chicano Youth Liberation Conference he sponsored in Denver in 1969, with delegates coming from many states, enthusiastically received Corky's blend of history and confrontation with the gringos.

Race often was invoked; sometimes to deny Indian inferiority, sometimes to proclaim La Raza as a Mexican-American community with its own especially meritorious history and culture. There was a search for roots outside the majority

American community, as in the black movement. Although some Mexican-Americans had little enthusiasm for identification with the bloody ancient Aztecs, to say so was not convenient when such enthusiasts as Luís Valdés were declaring that "La Raza . . . is the Mexican people" and that assimilated Mexican-Americans were "ex-raza."

The ambiguity of the term La Raza did not detract from its value as a rallying cry. But some Chicanos were carried away to the point where La Raza became a tie to all sorts of popular causes, even ecology. Stan Steiner claimed to have found a villager who declared, "I love to be poor," and interpreted that to mean that poverty symbolized the villager's "acquiescence to nature." That scarcely reflected the attitudes of poor farmers known to social workers and social scientists. Some Chicano ideologues romanticized villages and said that they would and must endure. Sociologists found no reason to believe that many of them would endure.

It was a common Chicano argument that their culture was being altered or threatened by Anglos, and required defense. It was argued that the Chicano culture was needed to improve the social position of Chicanos, a suggestion easier to state than to prove. There was much talk, in the fashion of the times, about cultural castration and genocide. There certainly could be little argument with the claim that Anglos were usually ignorant of Mexican and Latin civilization, or that their parading of a few such features as fiestas, rodeos, and regional dances was scarcely testimony to the contrary. There was an exceptionally active campaign to preserve the Spanish language.

It became a common stance of Chicano leaders and their supporters in the Anglo community that "cultural pluralism" was valuable. It proved much easier to state a general argument for that proposition than to posit specific gains to be expected. Furthermore, history suggested that it was difficult to achieve true cultural pluralism and that its values were difficult to measure. These were unpopular suggestions in the intellectual world, no doubt in part because they were difficult to refute and because intellectuals found vulgar the intuitive popular fear of an "excess" of pluralism.

Chicano leaders who used confrontation tactics offended or frightened not only Anglos but some of the older generation of Mexican-Americans. Some leaders talked of revolution, though it was not clear what they meant by it, even when demonstrators chanted solidarity with a long-dead Che Guevera. And although the Brown Berets of East Los Angeles, and the serape-clad members of MAYO (Mexican-American Youth Organization) in San Antonio, with their upraised clenched fists, provoked some fears of militarized chicanismo, they came to nothing. It could only be hysteria that led to some trepidation at the sight of high-school Chicanos occasionally draped in the crossed cartridge belts of the Mexican Revolution of 1910–1917.

Chicano poets, novelists, journalists, and playwrights have given spirit to the movement, as when Philip Ortega in a story in 1968 told of a leader whose words "straighten the spines of the forgotten people." And there has been much celebration of Chicano culture, but it usually has not been clearly defined. Some of the Chicano literature is as much a reaction against discrimination and poverty, or an expression of current intellectual and artistic trends, as it is specifically Mexican-American. That is the case with praise of Hispanic "collaborative action" being considered superior to Anglo individualism, a notion without historical foundation. Or the story by Génaro González (1970) that found a "natural freedom" that was superior to the "castrate freedom of societies," a romantic notion that far antedated chicanismo. It is trendy to sneer at the bourgeoisie, especially new Chicano entrants, who have moved to the suburbs and called themselves Spanish.

The impact of the Chicano movement has been considerable in civil rights, literary, artistic, entertainment, and journalistic circles; in some churches; and among academicians. But many Anglos have given only grudging attention; possibly a majority have given none at all. This is in line with the long-time Mexican-American complaint that they've received too little publicity and have been "hidden" from the public; and the movement has improved public attention. It has helped get more aid from government as well as public support against police brutality. It has helped get more teaching jobs for Mexican-Americans and introduced Chicano studies programs in universities. At the least it has publicized the problems of Mexican-Americans; at best it has urged these people to work more effectively in their own behalf.

Work and Labor Unions

Fury often runs deep with regard to the status of disadvantaged labor. Leaders of such groups, and their sympathizers, find it infuriating when people are optimistic about progress. On the other hand, "outsiders" are exasperated by unwillingness to acknowledge improvements as significant. It is the old story of the bottle being at once half empty for the pessimist and half full for the optimist. And the constant addition of immigrants makes the measurement of progress a matter for debate.

Average income levels for Chicano families are lower than for Anglos but higher than for blacks. In 1960 Mexican-Americans annually earned less than one-half the Anglo figure. In 1970 the median income of Mexican-American families was $7,120, which was 30 percent less than the income of all white families (including Mexican-Americans), and 13 percent more than black families. Chicano earnings varied much by region, with income conspicuously low in Texas and high in California. Father Theodore Hesburgh, of the U.S. Commission on Civil Rights, in 1968 said that workers in the lower Rio Grande Valley were treated like peons or slaves.

Chicanos find it especially difficult to become owners of enterprises, except at a petty level. They lack capital, good connections with monied Anglos, and they meet the view that

they are bad risks for loans. Yet they did make enough progress so that the first Annual National Symposium on Hispanic Business Enterprise could be held in 1978, sponsored
by the Department of Commerce.

While Chicanos welcome such attention and new investment aids from government and the private sector, they want
faster action. They naturally take the view that the bottle is
half empty. Low income obviously is damaging to the home
life, education, and general social status of Chicanos. The
movement is not interested in comparisons with incomes in
Mexico or Bangladesh, or with their own position of a few
years earlier. Nearly everyone is passionately interested in income; that will endure when Chicano poetry is forgotten.

Chicano workers are heavily represented in low-paying and
lowly regarded occupations. Despite an increase in the number of Chicanos moving to jobs demanding more skills and
offering more pay, the less desirable jobs have found many
recruits from unskilled Chicanos and the continuing stream
of migrants from Mexico. Mexican-Americans increasingly
have perceived illegal immigration from Mexico as being
especially damaging to themselves, and a factor that offset
some of the new aid given in the 1960s and 1970s. Many
Mexican-Americans cannot or will not compete with the
immigrants. An IRS survey found in 1975 that two-thirds of
the 48,000 illegally employed Mexicans interviewed earned
less than the $2.50 an hour, at a time when the average hourly
wage in the United States was more than $4.50.

Furthermore, although fewer than 10 percent of Chicanos
were in farm work by the late 1970s, that was much higher
than for Anglos or blacks; and the income and other working
conditions of rural workers were especially poor. Federal
minimum wages were only extended to agriculture in 1966,
and more than a decade later those wages are still less than
for non-farm work. By 1976 the agricultural minimum wage
was $2, which even with full-time employment did not give
enough annual income to keep the employee above the

federally designated poverty threshold. In addition, much farm labor is seasonal rather than full-time, and it is difficult to police widely scattered farm operations,

Chicano movement to better work has been slowed by continuing deficiencies in education and by discrimination in favor of Anglos for the better jobs. Also, differential wages are sometimes still paid for the same work, damaging not only to income and all who depend on it but a degrading badge of supposed inferiority. None of this has been much improved by urbanization. Indeed, not only is unemployment higher for Chicanos than for Anglos in town, but it is an especial source of concern that young Chicano suffer very high rates of un- and under-employment.

In the face of such formidable problems, the Chicanos—especially farm workers—have run into a barrier that has shattered the efforts of earlier immigrant groups; a lack of effective labor unions. Employer opposition to Chicano unions became especially frustrating in the 1930s and thereafter, when the labor movement in the United States generally became quite effective. The antilabor stance by employers of Chicanos and Mexican emigrants—especially in agriculture—increasingly seemed a glaring example of discrimination.

In addition, Chicanos have suffered discrimination from American unions. Some of it has been traditional labor objection to immigrant competition; some of it has been part of the effort to restrict membership in craft unions. In 1946 the "Brotherhood" of Railway Carmen only allowed Chicanos to work as common laborers on the Union Pacific. Some unions, it is true, were more enlightened; the International Ladies Garment Workers Union (ILGWU) in Los Angeles was an example, building on an enlightened tradition in the East regarding immigrant workers.

After World War II, Mexican-Americans elevated their complaints against such a condition and the Chicano movement began in important measure as a demand for effective labor organization and an end to exploitation. That was based not only on a sense of injustice, but on the Chicano's belief that he was a harder worker than the Anglo. That was a jolt for older Americans, who thought they had the original patent on the work ethic. Chicano efforts could be discounted as "coolie" labor, but that did not explain why they were so eager to move to skilled jobs and entrepreneurial activity.

So far as most job opportunities are concerned, significant improvement of Mexican-American pay and access has depended mostly upon their acculturation and assimilation. The civil rights movement of the 1960s and 1970s gave them some assistance in legislation, court action, and support by special groups and the public generally. Job discrimination was punished to some extent; jobs given to disadvantaged minorities were valuable to employers either in subsidies, in good will, or in government favor.

There was no evidence, however—nor could it be expected —that Chicanos improving their occupational and pay status would use it primarily to support chicanismo. Nor would the upwardly mobile Chicano form or join special Chicano labor unions in competition with the giants of the AFL-CIO or the Teamsters.

Chicanos in farm work were an exception. They often were immigrants, their work seasonal. They did need special unions, because none existed. The farm workers were a concentration of ill-paid persons, diffident and fearful, seldom more than feebly acculturated to North American society, and were little able or willing to change their status through acculturation. They lacked support in American society, unlike the members of craft and industrial unions. It was a tougher situation than that faced by Chicanos wishing to join the affiliates of the AFL-CIO. The problem of unionization of Mexican and Mexican-American farm labor thus has come to stand for many Americans as the heart of the total Chicano problem, which was far from the case.

Mexican-American farm unions had an unsuccessful history for more than half a century before the 1960s. But organizational costs were high since workers were scattered and often migratory. Low wages contributed to a vicious circle of inability to contribute to union funds and union inability to work effectively because of poverty. In addition, there were many potential strikebreakers in a poor population, either in the United States or in nearby Mexico. Labor solidarity could not be expected under such conditions unless some overwhelming spiritual inducement could be found— possibly in inspired leadership.

Furthermore, anti-union sentiment was strong in the Southwest, where labor organization generally proceeded more slowly than elsewhere. Law enforcement agencies listened to the employers, so that even association with union organizers was dangerous. The press generally was ignorant or biased against the farm workers of the Southwest. Even the provisions of federal labor law militated against successful organization among the farm laborers, who were excluded from coverage under the great labor reform legislation of the 1930s that set up the National Labor Relations Board. The result was that farmers were not required to recognize unions as bargaining agents, and only feeble instruments existed to use against farmers who engaged in unfair labor practices.

Organization of Mexican-American farm labor became more feasible in the 1960s for all of the reasons that led to the birth of the general Chicano movement then. In addition, agriculture was less important than before to the industrializing Southwest, so that farm pressure on government was somewhat lessened. The new labor movement captured the imagination of many Americans because Chávez, its most prominent figure, had that charisma then a staple of journalistic interpretation. Still, it often met with violence. In the late 1960s strikers were even arrested for praying in public!

In Chávez's grape workers strike in 1965, most of the big wine companies, owning huge vineyards, soon came to terms with the United Farm Workers; but the producers of table grapes did not. The boycott of the consumption of table grapes became a popular move in some civil rights and intellectual circles. Such sympathy was encouraged by the fact that then–California governor Ronald Reagan was a prominent conservative, so that to some observers the treatment of the UFW was part of a reactionary offensive on the West Coast. The California media often were quite unfair to the UFW in their treatment of the strike; but the movement did have press partisans in that state and elsewhere. The usual charges appeared that the UFW was "communist-inspired" or "-connected." That reinforced the view of some persons that a "McCarthyite" conspiracy existed against the UFW.

When the table-grape growers signed with the UFW in 1970, union members and supporters overestimated the effect on farm labor generally. The UFW received much aid from the AFL-CIO, but before long it faced a serious threat from the ambitious International Brotherhood of Teamsters, which had broken from the AFL-CIO. The Teamsters set out to capture control of the farm laborers, and Chávez spent years trying to hold together a part of the UFW against the giant Teamster organization. He eventually succeeded, and in the later 1970s the Teamsters abandoned their efforts.

By that time, however, the Chávez activity had diminished against the background of the much wider Chicano and civil rights movements. The 30,000 members of the UFW, plus their families, represented but a fraction of the Mexican-American community. Chávez set out to improve the efficiency of the UFW and to expand his operations. The temper of the times seemed favorable. Even "undocumented" Mexicans in the United States were becoming more militant. Many of the members of the UFW in the lettuce fields of the torrid Imperial Valley of California, near the Mexican border, were aliens—some commuting residents of Mexico—when on January 15, 1979 Chávez struck the lettuce fields.

It was the peak of the harvest season, so Chávez judged that a strike against eight (later eleven) of the twenty-eight major growers would force some to give in. That had happened in other strikes. It did not happen in this case. Chávez asked various sorts of compensation improvements of 40 percent and more; the owners offered 11 percent. Lettuce growers hired what they called "replacement workers," and the UFW called strikebreakers. The UFW members on the seventeen farms not declared closed by the union continued to work. The 4,300 UFW members on the strike naturally tried to prevent the use of the new workers. The owners tried to get the lettuce out, and some of them predictably hinted that a "revolution" was being planned by the UFW. There was no sign of that in Chávez's past record or in his present effort to raise the basic hourly wage of $3.70 for stoop labor.

Tension mounted, there was threat of violence, and finally on February 10, a UFW member, a citizen of Mexicali, Mexico, was fatally shot in a clash over replacement workers. Although law enforcement personnel were increased after that, the growers failed in their effort to get California governor Jerry Brown to send in the National Guard.

So the immediate strike was "lost," and the price of a head of lettuce went over one dollar to the consumer, a small matter compared with the price inflation for many items more critical and expensive. The growers, not the workers, gained.

The strike once again demonstrated the fact that foreign labor was being used in the country regularly and that it was available for strikebreaking. (By this time, some labor unions were cooperating with the Border Patrol in trying to control illegal immigration from Mexico.) A little calculation also indicated that a Mexican commuter might make on the order of $1,000 in a month or six weeks of labor in the lettuce fields of the Imperial Valley, a return immensely greater than could be gained for comparable (or most other) labor in Mexico. That dramatically indicated the difficulty of preventing illegal immigration.

If it could not be prevented, what served the growth of agricultural unions? At least, illegal immigration was more nearly a national issue than previously; possibly that would force a new approach to the problem.

One sign of the new importance of agricultural unions in California and national politics came in December 1979. The United Farm Workers union reached its first agreement with a grower that month after an eleven-month strike, with the state governor's office aiding in the process. Governor Jerry Brown was, at the time, a candidate for the Democratic party's presidential nomination.

School and Culture

Mexican-Americans have been badly disadvantaged in terms of education. The Coleman report of 1966 found achievement levels of Mexican-American children more than three grade-levels below whites of the urban northeast. They had poor schools, equipment, and teaching. The pupils suffered various physical and psychological problems due to poverty, prejudice, and discrimination and had to study what was essentially for many a foreign language. And Mexican-Americans were poorly prepared to meet such challenges. They came from a folk culture of illiterates in rural Mexico, so that home life and tradition urged schooling somewhat less strongly than with many Europeans. Chicano children, furthermore, often were needed as workers and were kept from school for that reason.

Much of the educational deficiency was due, however, to school segregation. As with blacks, Chicanos were segregated in schools for various reasons. This segregation went hand-in-hand with inferior facilities, partly a matter of penny-pinching by Anglos; but the latter also said that Chicano kids were stupid and would hold back and contaminate Anglos. Mexican-Americans and civil rights advocates in general opposed this segregation both for pedagogical reasons and because of the social effects of the practice. Some court rulings following World War II chipped at the practice. A great victory occurred in 1970 when a court held in Texas that Chicanos were a class covered by the famous *Brown v. Board of Education of Topeka* ruling (1954), which dealt with segregation of black children and held that such segregation by race, color, origin, or ethnic characteristics was prohibited. A court decision did not end segregated Mexican-American schools overnight, just as it had not done so with black schools.

Many Chicano children have had trouble with schooling in English, because Spanish has persisted more than most tongues brought by immigrants—partly because Mexican-Americans lived so much in isolation, partly because continuing immigration kept their numbers high. The large demand for Spanish language facilities is indicated by the existence of dozens of Spanish-language radio stations in the border states of the United States and by Spanish-language programs on TV in the Southwest. By 1978 Mexican-Americans in the Los Angeles school system outnumbered either Anglos or blacks, and half the kindergarten children spoke Spanish as their first language.

A pungent story illustrates the difficulties faced in the long Anglo effort to suppress Spanish in the schools. A little Chicano boy, as the story goes, asked the teacher in Spanish for permission to go to the toilet. The teacher insisted that he ask in English, and he kept squirming with his need and persisting in Spanish. Finally he said, "If you don't let me go, maybe I piss on your shoes."

So bilingualism was offered as a solution to the problem. It is claimed it would improve the general knowledge of Anglos and Chicanos, and teach a second language to both groups, valuable to individuals and to the nation. But there is argument over the idea. One group thinks it would be divisive and weakening to the nation, citing the nearby example of Quebec province, where the French-language issue has been entangled in arguments as to the political and economic relationship of the province with the rest of Canada. Another group wants bilingual schooling primarily to preserve Spanish, thus providing a Hispanic cultural enclave in the United States—exactly what some people fear.

The middle ground is occupied by those who say bilingual education would enrich the general culture, promote cultural pluralism, aid in the social adjustment of Spanish-speaking children, stop the penalization of Chicano children on IQ tests because such tests are given in a "foreign language," eliminate school dropouts due to lack of English, and help Chicanos in their search for employment. But the heart of the moderate argument is that bilingual education would aid in the learning process of all subjects, including English. The *New York Times* in a March 1978 editorial put it somewhat differently by stating that the intended purpose of bilingual education was "to hasten the transition from a foreign language to mastery of English." That, of course, raised the hackles of Chicanos who objected to Anglo cultural imperialism.

Some suggestions damage the idea of bilingualism. The most damaging asserts the possibility of more than one official language. The obvious difficulty is that people resist the idea in all countries, and it seldom has worked even moderately well when tried. There also is resistance to praise of "Pocho"—a mixture of Spanish and English—on the same grounds as rejection of praise for the spread of the black ghetto dialect as a "real language." There is little encouragement in vague Chicano claims that they were creating "our language," with influence from "the natural habitat." Nor can people take seriously the view that a Spanish accent in English is as acceptable as, for example, Senator Edward Kennedy's New England accent. One wonders what the Spanish Academy would think of that principle applied to Spanish.

In 1967 there were only a few bilingual programs in the United States, but by 1969 federal money was going to some 300, teaching Spanish to English speakers and English to

Spanish speakers. The government budgeted $150 million for 1979 for 564 bilingual education projects, enrolling 253,000 students, mostly Spanish speakers. Bilingual classes in Dade County (Miami), Florida, had considerable success, expressed in high school graduations and college enrollment. By the early 1970s the Los Angeles Police Department required police cadets to study Spanish. New York City and other municipalities have had similar programs affecting specialized personnel. It also has become common in some areas to post important signs and other public notices in both languages.

Critics have said that many of the bilingual programs are poorly conceived and badly executed. The evidence available merely suggests that the programs are not an automatic and universal panacea. The U.S. Office of Education, using 1975–1976 data, in 1979 found the programs of doubtful use. Supporters of the programs have said that it is too early to judge. Intuitively, it does seem reasonable that a reduction of language difficulty—if it is achieved—should improve learning. In any event, no public program of such size, and directed to the needs of the disadvantaged poor, will disappear in a flash. And even if its service to learning has proved modest, it has probably lifted the morale of Spanish speakers and led to better performance in English eventually. Surely, it has broadened the horizons of the English-speaking children who became involved. Experiment with bilingual education continued, as did controversy as to its justice and value. Even some Hispanic immigrants considered it the wrong way to attack the problem.

Many special training programs have been created to improve the learning and skills of Chicanos. Chávez gave training to his organizers. The Salinas, California, school board in the later 1970s supported a program, "English on Wheels," to teach farm workers better English for specific practical purposes. All sorts of student organizations were set up, with cultural and social programs with a Mexican-American orientation. The enthusiasm of Chicano youth for this development was expressed in March 1968 when some Los Angeles high school students struck for a larger Chicano content in the curriculum. Misguided arrests of student leaders for "conspiracy" to impede the educational process scarcely accomplished more than an increase in demands for "community control" of the schools.

Universities have scoured the country for Chicano (and black and female) students and faculty, also founding Chicano studies programs, with the mixture of useful and dubious results noted of Black Studies programs. There certainly is support for a balanced view of the cultural heritage of the United States, but how to define it? Regional peculiarities in the teaching of history, for example, have long been evident. There has been complaint that Chicano studies do not lead to jobs, but partisans believe it more important to foster pride in Chicanos and to sensitize the American public to their heritage. Attacks on the programs, therefore, have been ascribed to prejudice, as when Dr. Jesús Chavarría, founder at the University of California (Santa Barbara) of the first Chicano studies program in the country, was denied tenure in 1976.

The growth and new self-assertiveness of the Mexican-American community even seems to have affected the Roman Catholic Church. When in 1972 the First Encuentro of Hispanic Catholics in the United States was held, there was only one Hispanic bishop in the country; when the Second Encuentro was held in 1977, there were eight. Some groups in the church in the United States have fostered improvements in the lives of Mexican-Americans, and individual churchmen have even promoted chicanismo. But it does not seem likely that Mexican-American ideas or tactics will be much affected by the church.

Home and Social Life

Although Chicano militants have asserted the fundamental differences between the social life of their community and that of Anglos, there is some doubt about specifics. That Mexican-

Americans are family-oriented is an old staple of discussion. Such an orientation is based partly on peasant tradition, promoted by rural isolation and the usefulness of children as workers. Family orientation also is promoted by the life of alienation and oppression Mexican-Americans lead in the United States. But the size of Chicano families has declined in the United States with urbanization and acculturation.

Chicano writers have also found proof of strong family affection in extended families living under the same roof. But it gradually has become clear that such combinations often were merely the result of poverty, because prosperous—and some not so prosperous—Chicanos prefer one-family residence units. Even marriage ties outside the group have become more common than some Chicano literature allows. Naturally, such marriages most often occur with those culturally assimilated into the general society.

Segregated slum residence is a badge of the disadvantaged —sheds and tents in migrant farm camps, shacks in the villages and on the Anglo commercial farms, ramshackle apartments and huts in the barrios of Los Angeles and El Paso. A mountain of reports describe the dirt, lack of hot water, outdoor privies, and mounds of garbage. A Chicano writer has described the barrios as "pockets of poverty, tin-can alleys, and rat nests." A University of Texas study in 1968 pointed out that half of the houses in the lower Rio Grande Valley lacked plumbing or hot water—that is, they were like the shacks just across the river in Mexico. The Chicano movement echoed the strictures of earlier ghetto reformers against high rents for such slums.

Housing segregation is due not merely to poverty, but is imposed by Anglo determination to keep the Chicanos away, except when working (sometimes) or when spending money in certain types of Anglo business establishments. The usual rationalizations are offered: Mexican-Americans prefer to live apart; they are poor because they are lazy, ill-educated, and improvident; and besides, their lack of culture, bad habits, and dirt and disease must not be allowed to contaminate the children and women of decent folk.

But there is more to housing segregation than that. There sometimes is segregation between foreign-born and American-born Mexican-Americans. And segregation between Mexican-Americans and Anglos is not as great as that between Anglos and blacks. Furthermore, some segregation is based more on income level and social class than on an ethnic basis.

So Mexican-Americans live in the barrios; those of Los Angeles by the end of the 1970s contained 1.5 milion people, possibly larger than any city in Mexico but the capital. In Mexico, barrio has been a neutral name for city section; rich barrio, or poor; *barrio rico, barrio pobre.* But in the United States it stood first for home, then meant ghetto, and with the Chicano movement sometimes became "my turf, you bastards."

Mexican-Americans long have not drunk, worshipped, or danced with Anglos. Often they could not eat in an Anglo cafe or buy cigarettes there. The civil rights movement weakened but did not eradicate that type of segregation. Another type of segregation—in clubs and associations—has weakened with acculturation and Mexican-American self-assertion. Mexican-Americans long have had their own social, business, and religious associations. But recently there has been some shift of Mexican-American from exclusively Mexican-American to general American organized groups.

As with income improvement, pessimists see social integration far from being achieved, and they are right; and optimists see it as having come a considerable way, and they are right, too.

Law Enforcement Agencies and Mexican-Americans

Unfair, sometimes brutal treatment by public authority is a major Mexican-American complaint. The worst offenders are law enforcement officers, but they are backed by Anglo judicial and other authority and public opinion. One abuse is preferential attention and harassment: "What'r doin' here, bub?" The apprehension of illegal migrants is constantly conducted in a heavy-handed way, interfering with the rights of Mexican-Americans, who too often are harassed or illegally arrested. Labor conflicts often bring a rush of attention from local and state police, sheriffs, and an assortment of enthusiastic deputies. Attempts at labor organization in the Imperial Valley in the 1930s brought violence. Mexican-Americans then, and on many other occasions, suffered arbitrary arrests for the old standbys of police and judicial harassment: vagrancy, trespass, disturbing the peace, loitering, resisting arrest. Employers and other supporters in the Anglo community not only gave orders to the police but attempted some vigilante work of their own, some of it through American Legion posts.

This ugly history was summed up in 1968 by the U.S. Civil Rights Commission as "evidence of wide-spread patterns of police misconduct against Mexican-Americans in the Southwest." That report, and the rest of the civil rights movement, did something to correct the abuse; but it was far from eliminated.

Many sad cases occurred thereafter. In September 1975 Police Chief Frank Hayes of Castroville, Texas, arrested twenty-six-old Richard Morales, a Chicano, on suspicion of possessing stolen property. He took Morales to an isolated spot and shot him, by accident, Hayes claimed. A jury of eleven whites and one black found Hayes guilty of aggravated assault. He was sentenced to ten years, eligible for parole after twenty months. His wife, accused of burying the body 400 miles from the crime, pleaded no contest to a charge of tampering with evidence and was placed on probation for a year.

The Morales family lawyer said the case showed racial bias. In February 1977 the Justice Department in Washington ordered an inquiry, which seemed to change the department's practice of not prosecuting individuals for offenses already tried in a state or local court, "unless the reasons are compelling." Up to 1977 they seldom had been found compelling. But in September 1977, Hayes, his wife, and sister-in-law, were convicted by a federal court of violating the victim's rights, the only charge the federal government could make even though murder had occurred.

Joe Campos Torres, twenty-three, in 1978 was taken to a police station in Houston after being beaten by police at an isolated spot. The sergeant refused to book Torres and ordered him taken to a hospital. But he was later found drowned where he had been beaten. Two of the police officers were convicted of negligent homicide—one-year sentence suspended! The Justice Department in Washington said the sentence was inappropriately mild. That by itself would do little to protect Mexican-Americans.

Mexican-Americans and Politics

It has always been obvious that the best road to improvement of Mexican-American life was through politics. But to blast through the roadblocks erected by Anglos has required self-assertion, organization, and courage. Such roadblocks included gerrymandering, registration chicanery, intimidation at the polls, interference with meetings, and control of the press. Those problems could not be handled by the early voluntary associations of Mexican-Americans, which seldom had a political orientation before World War II. Mexican-Americans lacked money to back political action, and they lacked influence in economic and social life. In addition, Mexican-American strength was badly fragmented, sometimes scarcely organized beyond the neighborhood. Mexican-Americans only became evident as a national political factor during their 1960 "Viva Kennedy!" effort and even then were not an impressive factor.

Many things have led eventually to a workable combination of the qualities needed for movement of Mexican-Americans into politics: the civil rights movement, better education, the Chicano movement, a better position in organized labor, and assimilation—all of which have provided men and women of Mexican origins, some of them lawyers, who are capable of dealing with Anglos on their own ground. Political activity also has been promoted indirectly by President Carter's emphasis on international human rights, because it was possible to point out contradictions between his human rights position and the treatment of America's own "internal colony" of Mexican-Americans.

The results of Chicano political action have often been so poor as to be embarrassing, and it has had to be explained that many Mexican-Americans are not citizens, or that many are too young; but it is clear that many simply do not want to get involved. The problems are not felt uniformly in all areas, so that generalization is difficult. But the increase in citizenship and number of voters is bound to make it progressively more difficult for Anglo politicians to ignore Mexican-Americans.

Many Mexican-American groups have played some role in American politics. The United League of Latin American Citizens (LULAC) was founded in Texas in 1929 to defend itself against Ku Klux Klan violence, emphasizing loyalty to the United States. After World War II it enlarged its aims to include equality for Mexican-Americans, and it became a civil rights organization; but it was not politically militant. In California, the Mexican-American Political Association (MAPA), founded in 1958 to endorse candidates for office, among other functions, had considerable influence. MECHA (Chicano Student Movement of La Raza) engaged in some political action in several states. The Political Association of Spanish-Speaking Organizations (PASSO) in the early 1960s elected a city government in Crystal City, Texas, by joining with other groups, including the Teamsters Union and the Bishops Committee for the Spanish-Speaking; but the Anglos soon regained control.

The Chávez United Farm Workers in the 1970s mounted useful registration drives. A promising organization was the Mexican-American Legal Defense and Educational Fund, based in San Francisco. In 1973 Vilma Martínez, a law graduate (1967) of Columbia University, became president and general counsel of the organization. She was a well-known Mexican-American in the civil rights movement. Ms. Martínez took the view that with time and education the influence of Mexican-Americans in politics was bound to rise. She believed in working within the system, but not with humility.

La Raza Unida, of Texas, possibly the best-known Chicano political group, had limited success in getting Mexican-Americans elected; but it helped politicize them. It got control of Crystal City, Texas, and gained considerable publicity in 1977 when Crystal City became the only community in the state to refuse outright to pay state-sanctioned price increases for natural gas.

Some other potentially significant political groups drifted into blind alleys. Corky González of Denver wanted power for his people, but there was no reason to suppose his so-called "nation" of Aztlán ever would exist in a meaningful way. Nor did the future seem promising for López Tejerina of New Mexico and his idea of "free towns." It was not helpful to his chances for political influence in the United States when the Mexican leftist magazine *Proceso* stated (February 6, 1978) that López Tejerina called the "frontier of the United States a future war zone" in the independence movement.

The small crops of electoral offices reaped disappointed Mexican-American political leaders. In California, for example, the large Mexican-American population could not win a state office for their candidates, while blacks, fewer in number, could. But all blacks are citizens, while many Mexican-Americans are not; and many more Mexican-Americans than blacks are too young to vote.

Mexican-Americans elected their first member to the Los Angeles City Council in 1949 but in 1978 had no members on that body. In 1964 they elected their first mayor in the state, and in 1973 their first state senator. The possibilities of local action were seen when the city council of little Parlier, California, refused to appoint a Chicano police chief in 1971, whereupon aroused Chicanos won control of the city council the next year. Less publicized but indicative of grass-roots progress was the fact that Mexican-Americans elected their first member of a school board in California in 1953 and by 1978 had 120 seats on California school boards.

Mexican-Americans have traditionally comprised a larger percentage of the population in New Mexico than in California. There were two Mexican-American national senators from New Mexico, one in the 1930s and 1940s and one in the 1960s and 1970s. In the 1970s the first Mexican-American in half a century was elected governor of New Mexico. At the same time, another was elected governor of Arizona. Also revealing of changing conditions was the election of five Mexican-Americans to the eleven-member San Antonio, Texas, city council in 1977.

Since the Supreme Court ruled in 1973 that at-large representatives (as opposed to single-member districts) in states, cities, and school districts discriminated against minorities, a quiet revolution has been going on in various places. In parts of Texas it has meant the election of much larger numbers of Mexican-Americans and blacks.

Although such victories were far from giving Mexican-Americans their proportionate share of office, they showed that there was no reason to despair. The new day seemed especially marked by the appointment in 1977 of Leonel J. Castillo as the first Mexican-American chief of the federal Immigration and Naturalization Service, an agency long disliked by many Mexican-Americans.

These gains may prove to be short-lived, however, for, in April 1980, a U.S. Supreme Court decision overturned a U.S. Court of Appeals ruling that at-large elections were an unconstitutional barrier to black political participation. This Supreme Court decision was at once widely interpreted to permit a return to at-large elections where district elections had been substituted under court order.

Mexican-Americans as a Bridge?

Can Mexican-Americans serve as a bridge to Mexico, or even to Spanish America generally? Some of them claim that their cultural background fits them for such a role. A group of nine Mexican-American leaders apparently had something a bit different in mind when they met with Mexico's President López Portillo in January 1978 and offered to lobby for Mexico against President Carter's proposal to control illegal Mexican immigration. López Portillo praised the Mexican-American movement but declined to interfere in the internal affairs of the United States. A member of the delegation reportedly said on that occasion that Mexico should "use us as Israel uses American Jews," and as "Italy uses Italian-Americans."

That suggested a problem of divided loyalties. Even more damaging to the bridge idea, however, was the historical record of immigrant groups in the United States: with few exceptions, they had not been a vital factor as bridges to the old homelands. Neither strategic nor economic decisions usually have been much affected by ethnic group pressures, although much ostentatious attention has been paid to their opinions.

A less ambitious "bridge" notion is that a more prosperous, better educated, and more influential Mexican-American community would improve the Mexican—and Spanish American —view of the United States. No one can guess how much—if any—effect that will have on great affairs of state.

Another claim is that the influence of a better-treated Mexican-American community on United States culture would improve American ability to understand the Hispanic world. The results of that also are difficult to estimate.

What led Governor Jerry Brown of California in the late

1970s to declare his understanding that Mexico and the United States were "inextricably linked" and that disasters to one had to be felt by the other? Some role must be assigned the fact that he has had a large Mexican-American constituency. It also appears that he had high hopes of siphoning Mexican oil into California. Critics point out that he seemed to be encroaching on the foreign relations field reserved to the federal government. Other commentators say that the governor apparently was willing to move from the state to the federal sphere of activity.

One outcome is certainly conceivable: if Mexican immigration continues at a high rate and assimilation slows appreciably, the Mexican-American community might become a bridge carrying serious discontent between the countries. If that happens, they would be part of a "special relation" or "bridge" that no sensible person wants to exist.

EIGHT

Economic Dreams and Realities

Economics is at the heart of relations between Mexico and the United States. There are people in both countries who understand that a well-developed Mexico would have a much greater economic exchange with the United States than it has now, to the advantage of both. Truly drastic changes in economic ties will be difficult to arrange, however, both because vested political and economic interests will object and because the two countries are so mismatched in economic and social development. The balance of payments favors the United States, which Mexico resents; but perhaps the new oil exports will help enough to satisfy them south of the border. But it is unlikely. The import of Mexican vegetables draws angry American farmers to the border crossings to blockade shipments. Suggestions that the United States has to let in more Mexican manufactures draw almost irresistible objections from organized labor and industrialists. Mexico needs private investment capital but impedes its entry in many ways, rejects American suggestions that loosened regulation would help, and replies that it would prefer low interest loans, paid for directly or indirectly by the American government—that is, taxpayers. So that raises the question: How much does the American public want to pay for Mexican development? And just as difficult is the question of how much more aid Mexico could use effectively.

Payments and Nationalism

Mexico's balance of payments with the United States long has been unfavorable. Essentially, Mexico's shipments of raw materials are of less value than its imports from the United States, primarily of manufactured goods. Mexico also ships out money in profits from United States corporate affiliates operating in Mexico, and in interest on American loans and investments. These and other flows to the United States are only partially offset by American tourism. The imbalance is the more serious for Mexico because its trade with the U.S. is some 60 percent of all Mexican foreign trade. As a result, Mexico wishes to improve its access to the American market. The United States, on the other hand, carries on only about 4 percent of its total world trade with Mexico; so the importance of the Mexican share does not loom large in Washington.

The United States has been Mexico's major trading partner since the late nineteenth century. Commodity exchanges between the two countries surpassed $9 billion in 1978; the United States sent almost $4 billion worth of machinery, parts, chemical products, and finished metals in exchange for Mexican food, raw materials, minerals, and manufactures. By late 1976, this pattern produced a $2 billion trade balance in favor of the United States; but the gap narrowed to less than $200 million in 1978 as a result of increased Mexican oil exports. The current account deficit of over one billion dollars may increase, however, with rising profit remittances and necessary purchases of capital and petroleum equipment. If United States trade patterns or policies shift dramatically against Mexico, the latter's oil cannot cover the resulting trade deficits.

Unfortunately for Mexico, its imbalance with the United States is only part of a generally unfavorable Mexican situation with regard to international payments. Mexico's imports, largely for equipment, technology, and raw materials to operate and expand its industrial plant, have simply been allowed to outrun income from exports. In addition, Mexico has borrowed large sums abroad to finance its imbalance in commodity exchange, to pay for a variety of projects that give no immediate return (e.g., electric power), and to service the foreign debt. The Echeverría administration from 1970 to 1976 ran up the international debt to unprecedented levels and left the new president, López Portillo, to sort out the mess.

The external public debt went from about $2.2 billion at the end of 1967 to $9.8 billion at the end of 1974, to $20 billion at the end of 1976, and reached about $25 billion in 1978. In the years 1967–76 the external debt rose from 11 to 21 percent of the gross domestic product. The situation was such in 1978 that the government borrowed $8 billion abroad, but $5 billion went to service foreign debts.

These practices led to severe inflation in Mexico and forced in 1976 a devaluation of the currency for the first time since 1953. It also caused a loss of confidence among public and private investors and among businessmen generally. Pessimism also resulted from the fact that the generally good Mexican economic growth record since 1940 was not maintained. In 1976 production rose only 3.2 percent, which was less than half of the average growth per year since 1940. It also was less than population growth, so that per capita production actually declined. And 1977 was even worse, while improvement in 1978 was modest.

Echeverría devised a method of escape that he promoted in the United Nations: the Third World would control the prices of world exports and imports. Understandably, the developed countries resisted this extreme expression of the Third World desire for assistance. Echeverría's relations with the United States were not warm enough for him to make an effective effort to get concessions there. His successor could and did try, but with moderate success by the fall of 1979. Washington had its own economic problems, including inflation and big deficits in international accounts.

The devaluation of 1976 at the end of the Echeverría term, and other measures taken after December 1976 by López Portillo, did reduce the deficits in foreign trade and in the national budget, and somewhat lowered inflation. It also appeared that new petroleum exports soon would greatly relieve the situation if spending could be kept down. But it was irritating to Mexico to be required by the International Monetary Fund, as the price of aid, to exercise a fiscal restraint imposed from outside.

That the restraint came from outside, as did pressures from the United States, pricked Mexican pride, ambition, and desire for more freedom of action—in short, the spirit of nationalism. Deficits in the billions stimulated extreme nationalists and demagogues in Mexico to make wild charges with little regard for fact. In both Mexico and the United States, responsible interest groups naturally used national interest as one basis of their arguments. The calmest of political leaders bent to the winds of asserted national interest and danger to the fatherland; leaders in both countries feared political repercussions if they made concessions. Mexico declared that it merely wanted fair treatment by greater access to United States markets for its exports, but it maintained strict barriers of its own against the import of many types of goods that were manufactured in Mexico. The United States posed as a world leader of lower trade restriction but kept out many Mexican goods. Charges of insincerity on both sides were spread through the constituencies of leaders and over the waves of television.

Exchange of Commodities and Services

The goods, investments, and services exchanged between Mexico and the United States naturally reflect their resources. Mexico has subsurface resources and tropical crops that the United States wants, customers for American manufactured goods, fine beaches and interesting Indian relics for tourists, and opportunities for investment in a developing country. But Mexico wants to be less a supplier of raw materials and more an exporter of finished goods—that is, a fully industrialized nation. It is even wary of its new petroleum surplus, and as soon as it can build facilities wants to ship much of it as refined products.

Commodities

The tropical agricultural products the United States imports from Mexico include coffee, sugar, sisal, fruit, and cacao. Since the United States does not produce most of these tropical agricultural items, there is no cause for problems, so long as two conditions are met. First, Mexican prices and quality must be competitive. Second, other things being equal, Washington must not favor one tropical country over another. The tropical nations watch that closely, especially in connection with commodities in which there are frequent surpluses, notably coffee and sugar.

It is a different matter with Mexican crops that compete with United States producers—strawberries, citrus fruit, tomatoes, other vegetables, and meat. American producers resent the competition. They put pressure on members of government at all levels. They also strive to gain public sympathy for a variety of protests. A striking example occurred in early March 1978, when farmers blocked traffic at the international bridge at McAllen, Texas, to stop trucks bearing farm produce from Mexico. Police arrested about two hundred fifty of the farmers, whereupon many others converged on the lower Rio Grande

Valley to protest. Much of the activity in the area was organized by American Agriculture, a group hopeful of arousing farmers on a national basis. News pictures showed policemen forcibly detaining farmers in overalls.

In view of such opposition, it may be doubted that much will result from the commercial treaty signed by Mexico and the United States in 1977, the first between them since the agreement of 1942, which ran out in 1950. The 1977 agreement only provides for about $100 million more per year in trade, but it involves tariff concessions on both sides, more by the United States than by Mexico. This is in line with international suggestions that concessions on tropical products by industrialized nations is a useful way of helping development. In this case it includes fruits and vegetables and other agricultural products. Although the amount of trade is not large, it brought objections from American farmers.

In March 1980, the Commerce Department again replied to the petitions of Florida farmers that the prices of winter vegetables from Mexico were not fair. The department rebuffed the petitions. That was, of course, bad news for Florida farmers and good news for North American consumers and Mexican farmers. It was good news also for President López Portillo, who had been refusing to sign a new commercial agreement with Washington.

Mexican minerals have been important to the United States since the later nineteenth century, both for export to the United States and as a focus for investment. Lead, zinc, and sulphur are among those still of strong interest; also of actual or potential importance are deposits of copper, iron, and silver. Although Mexico in the 1970s began the nationalization of ownership of Mexican mining, foreigners were allowed to retain some interest. It became a favorite claim of Mexican nationalists that huge hidden Yankee ownership in minerals was a threat to Mexican control and policy. Finally, the American interest in Mexican petroleum in the early twentieth century that had died as other producers became important and as Mexico nationalized the industry, was revived in the 1970s.

Mexico buys a copious amount of American manufactures, especially producer goods to build her own manufacturing facilities. She closely restricts imports to Mexico of some manufactued products where Mexico has producing capacity: for example, textiles, clothing, television sets, refrigerators, and automotive vehicles.

The examples given are seldom competitive with American products in quality or price, but they sometimes are. In any event, large quantities of such items are bought by Mexicans in U.S. border towns and smuggled into Mexico, which would like to stop that traffic and integrate the border area more closely into the national economy. Mexico has, however, since 1966 created a special problem for itself in the border area. Its government encourages U.S. corporations to lease land in Mexico's border cities, there to import raw materials free of duty as long as the finished products are exported to the United States, where some of them are bought by Mexicans and smuggled into Mexico. The lure of these "in-bond" plants to American manufacturers is the same as in Hong Kong and Taiwan—cheap labor. By 1977 there were more than six hundred such plants just south of the Mexican border, assembling such items as radios, electronic equipment, pharmaceuticals, and clothes. Some of America's best-known corporations thus carry jobs to Mexico, as American organized labor complains; and Mexico derives income from wages, taxes, and the sale of supplies and services.

While Mexico faces the problems of large Mexican purchases in United States border towns, smuggling from the United States and other countries, and in-bond plants, it wants the American market opened to many Mexican manufactures. American unions and manufacturers say no. The ILGWU, for example, which protected Chicano workers in Los Angeles, has lost much membership because imports of garments from the Far East and Latin America are made by workers whose wages sometimes are only one-tenth of those of ILGWU members. If the United States opens its markets wider to such low-cost producers, either on political or economic grounds, ways must be found to compensate or appease American workers.

Investment

There is a sizable American investment in Mexico on the order of $4 billion, which is more than 70 percent of total foreign investment in the country. It is not large by American standards, but important to those involved, who are ready to spring to the defense of their interest. And such defense is necessary because Mexican nationalists say that American investment is a threat to their independence. That, at least, misleadingly ignores the fact that some 90 percent of all investment in Mexico is Mexican, which is a far cry from the days before the Revolution of 1910–1911, when half of investment in Mexico was foreign. Foreign investment in Mexico today is even less than it was when rapid industrialization began there during World War II, and the economy now is enormously larger than it was then. The present proportion of foreign investment has not changed significantly for some years and probably will not, if for no other reason than intense Mexican interest in the matter.

Mexican nationalists assert that foreign investment is larger than the official figures because dummies in Mexico hide some foreign holdings, especially when foreigners gain control of enterprises that by law are to be Mexican-controlled. That certainly underplays the brilliant success of Mexico's efforts to push foreigners out of many sectors of the economy: for example, banking, insurance, primary chemicals, automotive vehicles, minerals, petroleum, electric power, and railways. That policy of Mexicanizing (majority local ownership) or nationalizing (total Mexican ownership, by the state or by private funds, or a combination of the two) drove foreign investment almost entirely into manufacturing, and only into portions of that sector.

Mexican critics are fertile in arguments. They find that some foreign investment in manufacturing is in "strategic" lines that give foreigners critical leverage in the economy. In this argument, statistics scarcely matter. Equally imaginative is the use of statistics to show that a majority of Mexican industries are not *totally* owned by Mexicans. They sometimes complain that profit remittances by foreign affiliates are greater than new investment; or even, simply, that profits are too high. There is complaint when American-owned enterprises sell only in Mexico. Also, when they sop up local investment funds instead of bringing them in from abroad.

There is no question that much complaint about foreign investment is political or emotional. Some Mexicans mistakenly suppose that it is clear that the country would be better off with no foreign capital. Others, with considerably more rationality, want capital only from international organizations. Many Mexicans, like most people in the world, are eager to assign their troubles to foreign devils.

The Mexican government and the official party try constantly—and obviously with less than total success—to put across the thesis that foreign investment is helping build a new Mexico. The government joins the critics, however, in complaining that foreign investment charges are exploitative. Proof on that subject often is irrelevant to political argument.

Such nationalist pressure, and common prudence in politics, have impelled Mexico to encourage more co-ventures between Mexican and foreign investors, with the majority share in Mexican hands. That "Mexicanization" does something to defuse nationalist cries. In any event, Mexico needs great sums of investment capital and the ruling party has emphasized this fact for decades. What is required is an even wider repertory of institutional arrangements to permit investment with a minimum of political repercussions. It is certain that intelligent leaders in Mexico and the United States will not advocate a return to foreign investment in Mexico without regulation.

Services

There are a number of service exchanges between Mexico and the United States. Tourism flows heavily both directions —labor largely from Mexico to the United States, and other exchanges flowing largely from the United States to Mexico. The largest flow to Mexico other than tourism involves technical and managerial personnel hired by Mexican firms or American affiliates in Mexico. The numbers of these have for a long time been limited by Mexico, but many still are required. The need for engineers is possibly more obvious than for managerial talent. But the latter is of critical importance to all developing countries. Mexico long has used not only American managers but American managerial methods, imported texts, and professors to spread the word. In addition, many Mexicans have gone to the United States for managerial experience and to study the theoretics of modern administrative methods.

Mexicans also have gone to the United States to study other subjects, often for advanced degrees in universities. Those subjects include economics, public and business administration, all sorts of engineering, and natural and computer science. Given the cost of higher education and the peculiar deficiencies of the universities of Mexico, this exchange is likely to continue for many years.

A small amount of exchange of persons occurs within some of the less populous occupations. There are a few international law firms in the two countries, with personnel transferring between both countries. American advertising agencies have been establishing branches or affiliates in Mexico for some years, and individual Yankees try their hand at it. Public relations as theory and practice has been exported from the

United States to Mexico and has struggled to establish itself there as a vocation separate from advertising.

In addition to scientific and technical personnel, the United States provides Mexico with technological processes, something a developing country badly needs. Mexico cannot afford the expense or provide the skilled personnel for an effective research establishment of its own. It knows that, but nationalists complain about the price of the imported technology in license fees and other charges, and about restrictions on the export of goods produced under license. These complaints, particular favorites of nationalists, have forced the Mexican government to make gestures toward control of profits made by foreigners from the sale of their science and technology. In fact, however, there is little that countries like Mexico can do about the problem except to try to play suppliers against each other, and gradually build up domestic scientific and technological capabilities. Since the latter is a difficult proposition, probably little will change for decades.

There has been some exchange in the movie industry— of players, directors, cameramen, capital, and technical equipment. Some Mexicans have been stars in Hollywood: Ramon Navarro, Dolores del Rio, Lupe Velez, Cantinflas, Katy Jurado. Mexico is a popular location for American movie companies: Elizabeth Taylor and Richard Burton at Puerto Vallarta for "The Night of the Iguana," as well as many western companies in the rugged country of Durango and other Mexican states. U.S. movies are immensely popular in Mexico and are shown with the original soundtracks and Spanish subtitles, a curious practice when compared with a smaller Spain, where nearly all foreign-language films are dubbed in Spanish. The large export of American films probably will continue as the Mexican film industry continues in the doldrums that have afflicted it for years—a situation apparently induced by the political bureaucracy. Experience in many countries suggests the improbability of rapid change.

The tourist exchange between Mexico and the United States is large and may grow much larger. For some years a rapidly growing tide of American tourists provided Mexico with lush income; indeed, at times this "industry without chimneys" has been a major element in the Mexican balance of payments. In 1978 some 3.5 million American tourists went to the interior of Mexico and spent about $1 billion; visitors to the border area left about $1.6 billion in Mexico.

However, that income from American tourism became increasingly offset by the loss of revenue resulting from Mexican tourism within the U.S. interior, as well as American border cities. That loss during 1978 totalled nearly $1.2 billion. The government of Mexico complained often about the situation but did little to alter it. The currency devaluation of 1976, however, made the peso so much less valuable in relation to the dollar that Mexican tourism and border transactions declined drastically. They began to recover, however, and Mexico would find it very difficult to keep them permanently depressed.

There is a large potential for further growth of American tourism in Mexico. A startling glimpse of what that potential might be is suggested by the fact that Spain (population of 35 million) in 1978 was host to 40 million tourists, and that was largely a development of the last two decades. There are about as many Americans and Canadians (260 million) panting to flee the snow to tropical Mexico as there are Europeans aiming at Spain. And Mexico has at least as many exotic "natives" and archaeological and architectural marvels as Spain. Furthermore, Mexico is much more reliably warm during the winter than the sunbelt of the United States.

Mexico is aware of this great potential, and public and private funds are constantly being pumped into new beach havens and other resorts. There is, to be sure, an old nationalistic outcry against a tourism that creates a nation of "bus- and shoeshine-boys"; this outcry conveniently overlooks the haughty headwaiters and well-paid hotel managers, to say nothing of chefs, car rental services, and tour operators.

This great tourism bonanza, that no other country in Latin America enjoys, is partly due to the nextdoor-neighbor position of Mexico. Not only is it relatively cheap to fly there, but Americans also can drive across the border. Proximity and convenience of travel to Mexico built that nation's tourist industry from almost nothing in the years after 1940. Travelers to Mexico—and to Spain—in the nineteenth century left accounts of vile inns and worse roads. Both have improved almost beyond recognition. Tourism has helped, requiring a big investment in highways, airports, hotels, and restaurants. Motels, then trailer parks, began to spring up. At border crossings quarter-mile lines of camper trucks belonging to tour clubs signaled the need for more entry points. Big American organizations found it convenient to alternate their convention sites between Miami Beach and Mexico City or Acapulco.

The attractions of Mexico have included not only beaches, but exotic food; folk art; jewelry and silver objects; bullfights; colonial palaces, churches, and monasteries; and a generally vibrant and cheerful foreign atmosphere. There are in Mexico more ancient pyramids than in Egypt. There are charming old colonial towns, such as Taxco, San Miguel de Allende, Oaxaca, and Morelia. And there is Mexico City, with well over 12 million inhabitants, apparently destined (or condemned) to be the largest city in the world.

Mexico also offers a stable political system and a well-policed environment for the tourist, who naturally is not looking for coups d'etat, revolution, civil war, rampant crime, or terrorism—all of which in recent years have badly damaged tourism in some countries. The growth of the Mexican tourist industry depends on the continuation of a social environment acceptable to the tourist. When in 1976 a few acts of violence against Americans were committed, and some U.S. publications and organizations badly exaggerated them, some over-sensitive Mexicans charged a "conspiracy" to wreck the tourist industry south of the border. This conspiracy charge was stimulated also by sensitivity about the Echeverría administration's poor relations with Washington, and nervousness about the problems distorting the Mexican economy. And finally, it was stimulated by the fact that in 1975 American Jews boycotted Mexico's tourist centers as a result of Mexico's vote in favor of a U.N. resolution equating Zionism with racism. Not even sales of margaritas and beach umbrellas were immune from political considerations.

Mexico's New Oil Power

Nothing is less immune to political considerations than oil; and suddenly Mexico had oceans of it.

Reserves and Production

As far as Mexican oil is concerned, the big drama has involved the figures on reserves. At the end of 1970 Mexico's proven reserves of hydrocarbons (oil plus natural gas) were 5.5 billion barrels; the official figure at the end of 1975 was 6.3 billion; at the end of 1976 it was 11.16 billion. By then excitement was in the air because many people in the oil industry, within and outside Mexico, had good reason to believe that new finds, especially in southern Mexico, were being underreported. Rumors circulated that Mexico was sitting on news of "another Saudi Arabia."

The government was unable to maintain its cautious attitude, or perhaps it simply was issuing news on a planned schedule. In any event, by 1977 the estimate of "probable" reserves of hydrocarbons in Mexico was 60 billion barrels, which was six times that of Alaska's North Slope. By early 1981 Mexico's official estimate of "proved" reserves was tripled from 20 to 60 billion barrels, with another 40 billion "probable" and total "potential" reserves (including proved and probable) of 250 billion barrels. Again the whispers were that Mexico would prove to be another Saudi Arabia; after all, careful oil exploration had covered only a small part of the country.

Production also rose. In 1973 daily production of crude oil averaged 470,000 barrels; by February 1977 it passed one million a day, and each day the equivalent of about 300,000 barrels of condensates and natural gas were being produced as well. By early 1981 daily production of crude oil and liquid gas was more than 2.2 million barrels. PEMEX (the national oil monopoly) planned to level off in 1982 at 2.7 million barrels a day, and to stay at that level for two years. At least that was what the Mexicans have said. But plans could change for apparently the oil can be produced at a much faster rate. A U.S. government study, released early in 1979, said that Mexican production could go to 3.8 million barrels a day within a decade; another put it at more than twice as high.

Mexico has suddenly changed from a net importer of petroleum to a sizable exporter. Its petroleum industry exports in 1976 were worth about $560 million. It expected daily exports of crude in 1977 to be at a daily average of about 200,000 barrels, worth nearly $1 billion. About 80 percent of Mexican oil exports went to the United States. By January 1979 that amounted to about 400,000 barrels a day, and the bill for the year might have come to more than $2 billion. Of course, that was only a small part of the total American consumption of 18.5 million barrels a day. By 1980 total exports reached a million barrels a day, resulting in an annual income of some $15 billion. And, by other PEMEX estimates, possibly a bit more than that by 1982, to which could be added $2 billion for exports of natural gas each year. Although the projected figures for 1982 would only bring Mexico's exports to about 2 percent of total world trade in oil, they have become immensely important to Mexico, of considerable significance to the U.S., and of some interest to all the Free World.

The Natural Gas Controversy

The new Mexican oil fields are also rich in natural gas, and the shortage of that fuel in the United States in the winter of 1976–77 suggested that Americans would be happy to import from Mexico. Plans were quickly laid for a pipeline. In August 1977 PEMEX signed a letter of intent with six American gas distribution companies whereby those companies would provide some of the financing. The price of the gas was set by a formula that came to $2.60 per thousand cubic feet, considerably higher than the price of Canadian natural gas. The line was to link pipelines at McAllen, Texas, with gas fields eight hundred miles away in southern Mexico. The line would carry 2.5 billion cubic feet a day, which compared with 2.2 billion handled by the trans-Canada line. But the Mexicans hoped to have their line in operation by late 1979, whereas the Canada line was expected to go on stream no earlier than 1982. These plans were boosted in September 1977, when the United States Export-Import Bank approved a $590 million credit for equipment for the pipeline project in Mexico, apparently seeing no fault in the price or anything else.

Some Mexicans, however, objected to the line as increasing dependence on the United States. The government replied that only leftovers from Mexican use would go to the Yankees. That appeasement of Mexico's nationalists went for naught, because Washington vetoed the price of $2.60 per thousand cubic feet. Over succeeding months the argument over the technical, economic, political, and supposedly moral aspects of the $2.60 price lost the interest of many observers. The Washington decision certainly had been to some extent influenced by the fact that natural gas pricing is a touchy matter, both for the public, and between Congress and the president as well.

The Mexican reaction was strongly nationalistic, and President López Portillo cancelled the plan for the pipeline to

Texas, asserting that Mexican industry would adapt from oil to natural gas. He was under heavy political pressure to make such a decision, whether or not he thought it economically sound. In early 1979 he said that Mexican natural gas would not be available for the United States, being used by Mexican industry, but reversed himself in September.

After months of negotiation, Mexico agreed to sell limited amounts of natural gas to the United States at $3.63 per thousand cubic feet, a price which would be adjusted quarterly. The 300 million cubic feet being pumped across the border is considerably less than the 2.5 billion agreed upon several years before and only a drop in the United States's daily 55 billion cubic feet consumption. Some citizens still resent what they call a "holdup," but others press for a reasonable compromises. Influential senators Frank Church (D.-Idaho) and Edward Kennedy (D.-Mass.) early in 1979 said they hoped that the U.S. government would settle the natural gas argument with Mexico. The symbolic September 1979 agreement only temporarily quieted them on this issue. The new Mexican petroleum age promises to present many more policy problems to the neighboring countries.

The Policies of Neighbors

The trouble with the game of "chicken" is that either one or both players may be badly hurt. In the petroleum contest between Mexico and the United States in the late 1970s it has not been just a question of economic muscle; political factors have been at least as important. Which leader would first feel inclined or compelled to make a concession? Would it be met in kind, or with obstinacy, or even escalated demands? Could simultaneous and offsetting concessions be arranged? The Mexican president has less room for economic maneuvering than his Washington counterpart, but does he have more political room in a country with a "one-party-dominant" system? At least, he hopes so. But Mexican policy focuses on the United States in a way that United States policy does not focus on Mexico. That alone makes decisions on petroleum exports to the United States more important to Mexico City than to Washington.

The U.S. president, in fact, has little political room for maneuver. Policy is made against a backdrop of trouble. In 1978 the American trade deficit soared to a record $28.5 billion, much of it due to petroleum imports, which had inexorably risen—or been allowed to rise—until they were about half of American oil consumption. In 1978 and 1979 American newspapers carried rueful cartoons showing the country begging for Mexican oil. Late in 1978 a National Security Council study found Mexican oil so important that it proposed enticements to Mexico: more imports of Mexican farm produce and textiles as well as establishment of quotas for Mexican immigrant workers.

That was too radical for Congress, some of whose members believed that the oil shortage was contrived by the oil companies to make big profits on foreign oil. Probably none of the congressmen approved of the enticements suggested by the NSC. Furthermore, despite the natural gas controversy with Mexico, that country's oil exports to the United States continued to rise. President López Portillo stated that the United States would continue to be the chief customer for Mexican oil, although he also said that Mexico wished to diversify its customer roster.

Energy Secretary James Schlesinger made another sort of suggestion in January 1979: since the United States now had a surplus of natural gas (despite the problems of two winters before), industry should temporarily (for six or seven years) emphasize use of gas fuel rather than coal. Having just made some conversions from oil to coal upon government urging, industry has not been attracted to another switch. Besides, it is not fond of short-term expedients.

One scheme has proposed that Mexican oil replace Alaskan on the West and Gulf coasts of the United States. That would require revocation of the prohibition on exports of Alaskan oil. The switch, so the argument runs, would raise Alaskan production slowed by West Coast oil gluts; and higher Alaskan output means lower prices. Cynics say that nothing means lower prices.

Yet another suggestion is a three-way swap of Alaskan oil to Japan in exchange for Mexican oil diverted from Japan to the American West Coast. That would save transportation charges, including those to the Gulf Coast via the Panama Canal for Alaskan oil. It also would raise Alaskan production. By early 1981 the Congress had not agreed on either scheme.

Another possibility, much discussed, has been to raise the price of U.S.-produced oil from the government-mandated average of $9 a barrel to the average of about $15 a barrel, paid in March 1979 for imported oil. Such a change has been considered with great caution by politicians, who are unable to find a sure formula for appeasing everybody. Oil companies would reap huge profits, unless they were heavily taxed, and consumer prices would go up. Could a way be found to compensate or appease the citizenry? It is not surprising that there was hesitation and contradiction in Washington. Nor is it surprising that Mexican leaders have concentrated on their own problems. López Portillo at the beginning of 1979 stated that oil output would be tied to the pace of Mexican development and not allowed to exceed the nation's ability to "digest" the income effectively, or to cause inflation. That is in line with the latest international thought on development, and it has met the fears of Mexicans engaged in the great oil debate.

The expansion of the oil industry has been enormously expensive, and that has worried some Mexicans. It appears that investment in various aspects of the industry will amount to $15 billion or more during the years 1977–82. Not only is crude oil production being increased, but Mexico is building refining facilities in order to increase the proportion of processed materials shipped. It also is pushing the petrochemical industry, a heavy user of capital.

Oil revenues also are tied to agriculture in Mexico. The

country has developed a growing deficit in farm output. Food imports in 1977 were up to $700 million, compared with $400 million in 1976. There were scary reports that they might go to $3 billion by 1982, which would be about half of the oil revenues expected in that year. A government official in 1978 had that in mind when he said that Mexico did not want to export oil and import food—which is what Venezuela and some other countries have done. López Portillo tried to calm such fears by stating that oil gave Mexico financial self-determination—that is, freedom to solve her own problems, including food production.

Such statements have been reassuring to nationalists, when they choose to believe them; but they do not assuage all Mexican fears, one being of famine. The country historically has suffered many periods of food shortage and skyrocketing prices. The recent peasant past of many Mexicans has locked in their breasts a belief that self-sufficiency in maize and beans is the only basis for prosperity. In the 1970s many people were unable to believe in arguments supporting food imports paid for with other commodities. Furthermore, some political leaders worked hard to appeal to this simple faith. That was the easier because runaway population growth was a specter visible to most Mexicans.

Mexico has not joined OPEC, apparently wanting independence of action; and why not, since it can receive OPEC, or higher, prices for its oil exports. Washington seems curiously optimistic about the value of this policy to American objectives, supposing that it would be damaging to OPEC. In any event, Mexico can join OPEC when it chooses, which would delight the other oil exporters.

With so much at stake, the rumor factories have been busy. Invention and trial balloons could scarcely be distinguished by the man in the street, and apparently not always by responsible officials. It was reported in January 1979 that Mexico was asking concessions for the export of 2,700 items, some to be let in free of duty charges. Even if a Mexican official made such a suggestion, he knew it to be an ostentatious bluff. An even more incredible report was that the huge Mexican oil potential was known in Mexico at the time of the 1938 expropriation but kept secret lest foreign capitalists get control of the country. It was supposed to have been confined to a group called "Guardians of the Secret." But the information on the southern Mexican oil fields was not available in 1938. Oil exploration is not done secretly with shovels. In addition, information of that magnitude could not be kept secret by a group. Finally, some statesmen before López Portillo would have been irresistibly tempted to exploit the "hidden" oil. However, the story is an interesting reflection of extreme nationalism in Mexico, where the protection of "nonrenewable natural resources" from Yankee imperialism is an article of faith.

At first glance one might have supposed that the Mexican petroleum bonanza would make the two countries better neighbors, but three or four years after the bonanza was revealed that no longer seemed certain.

Cost of the Immigration "Safety Valve"

There is no single formula for calculating the costs of Mexican illegal immigration to the United States. It depends on the assumptions allowed and the adopted conceptions of benefits and debits. Those conceptions are, at times, simplistic, with people making the common remark that "it costs the United States a packet." That usually means that the speaker is thinking of Social Security, welfare, and education costs; the expense of border patrols and installations; internal searches by the Immigration and Naturalization Service for aliens; deportation proceedings and shipments; and jobs and wages "taken" from Americans by alien workers. Some fairly firm dollar figures can be assigned to many of those factors, but it is more difficult to estimate costs in social division and unrest.

In either case, it is arguable that costs are outweighed by the productive activities of low-cost Mexican laborers, who work at jobs Anglos—and many Chicanos—will not take. It might even be suggested that costing include a guess at the value to the United States of a culture-group more driven by the work-ethic than the increasingly hedonistic and pension-oriented population of longer residence.

The dominant political thought in Mexico considers the value of the safety value to that country to be beyond question. Nationalist critics have to be assuaged, but they will not be allowed to make policy. In any event, it is unlikely that the Mexican government could do much to control migration at a cost it would be willing to pay. The pressure of population growth on workers simply is too great. Mexico cannot increase jobs or decrease population growth fast enough to permit much change in this situation for some time.

If Mexican population growth cannot be forced down, America may be needed as a safety value indefinitely—not an attractive prospect to the United States. That growth rate long has been well over 3 percent annually—one of the highest in the world, and more than three times that of the United States and the Soviet Union and higher than that of China or India.

From its present population of about 64 million, Mexico at current rates probably will reach more than 100 million in the year 2000, 200 million by 2025, and 400 million by 2050, incredible as that seems. Some people tell us that it cannot happen, that too many factors—famine, bourgeois prudence —must intervene to prevent it, but no one really knows. What has happened in the last forty years says it may happen.

There is an influential minority in Mexico that advocates population control. President Echeverría put himself on the side of "family planning," considered more acceptable to Catholic Mexico than "control" or the even worse, "prevention." There has been a small amount of progress, but it is not clear that much more can be achieved. Middle-class Mexicans in the cities conspicuously limit the size of their families. But poor farmers and workers have little reason to limit family size, indeed, often preferring to have as many workers in the family as possible. Change is especially needed in the huge bloc of poor peasants, which supplies the immigrants to the United States. For them, probably only economic improvement, education, and changes in values will much slow the birth rate.

Mexico's leaders say they favor a lower birth rate, preferring to export goods rather than workers. And the United States is invited to help by taking more Mexican commodities. So American policy and expenditures are tied to Mexican family life and that to illegal immigration.

On Helping Mexico's Development

It has been observed that many of the economic relations between Mexico and the United States are strongly—if not quite immovably—fixed in differential natural and human resources. The countries are vastly different in human resources because the institutional bases for their development have been so sparse in Mexico. History shows that human resources as molded by institutions—educational, moral, familial—usually are not easily altered. It is therefore best to assume that without some extraordinary measures, there will be no revolutionary change in economic relations between Mexico and the United States. It may be hoped that incremental changes may some day add up to significant gains.

If drastic measures are suggested, they will have to contend with the argument that year by year it is clearer that nations essentially develop themselves, that gobs of petroleum money, for example, may be indigestible and may distort a society rather than develop it. National development is one of the most complex of human endeavors, as much social and political as economic. It might be sensible to ask, Would a large-scale crash effort by the United States to help develop Mexico be realistic, or just a expensive dream?

If such drastic measures are suggested, there will be disagreement both within and between Mexico and the United States over what types are wanted. A part of that relates to "costs"—who will pay for change? While we might hope to enjoy a few delightful changes that cost no individuals or groups anything, there would be even more that cause dislocation and damage. Drastic changes in flows of commodities, services, or money could be expected to hurt someone in Mexico, the United States, or other countries. Presumably, special interests and individual laborers, employers, consumers, and taxpayers would retain their capacity to complain.

If Mexico is reluctant to settle for gradual improvement in economic relations with the United States, it can increase economic ties with other countries, but probably that would not be fruitful. Heavy, deliberate Mexican reordering of economic exchange with the United States almost certainly would hurt Mexico considerably. Furthermore, it is unlikely to find another country any more willing than the United States to finance rapid Mexican development.

Possibly Mexico could accept less rapidly improved trade with the United States if Washington more clearly acknowledged that proper understanding of Mexico's needs requires that the United States defer to Mexican knowledge of the Mexican culture. Also, a big comfort to both countries would come from an American decision to put some special resources to work for Mexican development on a more long-term basis. It need not be only money but could include such things as scholarships and regularly scheduled tariff reductions in Mexico's favor.

Such special treatment, particularly on tariffs, would meet a storm of criticism around the world. It might be best explained as a necessary special relationship with a next-door-neighbor, who was unavoidably exporting poverty to the

United States in the form of poor citizens. The nations would object but would secretly think it understandable.

There might be less sniping by politicians and others in the United States at such a program because it would be an agreed-upon long-term policy, so that the fundamental debate would not be required each year. If it was thus institutional-ized Americans might eventually think it as precious at the Monroe Doctrine or the Panama Canal. Also they might find that it makes good business.

The mind boggles at the thought of children in Boston and Bangor learning in school that improvement of the lives of our neighbors in Michoacán was what the Pilgrims had in mind all along. And the imagination simply cannot cope with the notion of Mexican youngsters in Querétaro and Oaxaca singing "God Bless America!" But we can hope.

NINE

Tasks of Diplomacy

The petroleum and immigration problems between neighbors touch in many places, a great web of issues and interests that often vibrates with tension. Some of the vibration results from the history of relations between the nations, especially as they remember slights or humiliations. National goals, molded by history, social structures, institutional aims, and nationalist passion and dreams, help determine international relations. A part also is played by diplomatic methods, in some measure standard for all modern states but also fashioned by the idiosyncracies of the national societies. There is plenty of diplomatic and technical skill on both sides, and no lack of will, so national interests seldom are sacrificed except under extreme pressure. Great diplomatic coups do not await cleverer foreign ministers or prettier packaging of bargaining points. One variant that can alter all calculations occurs when the perceived importance of issues oscillates, to the confusion of the predicters. Individual issues—such as petroleum, immigration, political orientation, or economic development—are part of a net of calculation, but the accuracy of the calculation is not known until the future has become the present. Who could have guessed in 1938 what roles petroleum and immigration would play forty years later in the relations between Mexico and the United States?

1821–1980: From Foul to Fair to What?

Recollection of earlier events colors relations today between Mexico and the United States. Those relations were very poor from Mexican independence in 1821 to the United States–Mexico war of 1846–1848; a bit better, but not warm, up to the time of the dictator Porfirio Díaz; considerably warmer during his regime (1876–1911); were fouled again during and after the Mexican Revolution, from 1911 to about 1940; improved considerably from then to the later 1960s, without being precisely genial; then in the 1970s began to cool again, so that it was not clear how they would develop in the 1980s.

Early relations largely revolved around territorial matters, with Americans moving westward and pressing into Mexican territory, and while American statesmen discussed changes in the boundaries, by one means or another. Mexico was understandably alarmed and made efforts to get help from France and Britain. Nothing sufficed and the feared disasters occurred. The acquisition by the United States of much territory claimed by Mexico soured relations after the annexation of the Texas Republic in 1845, the huge territorial concessions of the Treaty of Guadalupe Hidalgo in 1848, and the Gadsden Purchase of 1853. Those territorial losses are not forgotten in Mexico today.

From 1821 to the 1880s, the United States developed a bad opinion of Mexico, observing its political instability and poor economic and social development. American comments on Mexican "inferiority" did nothing to improve relations; nor were those relations improved by a few U.S. mutterings about gaining more territorial concessions from Mexico, even acquisition of the entire country. Somewhat counterbalancing this, some Mexicans after 1848 developed a mingled admiration and fear of rapid demographic and economic growth north of the border. But since economic relations between the two countries remained puny, there seemed to be no benefit likely for Mexico.

The continuing possibility of North American expansion at Mexico's expense was illuminated in 1859 when the government of Benito Juárez signed the McLane-Ocampo Treaty. It gave the United States a transit zone, useful for a canal, in the Mexican Isthmus of Tehuantepec and the right to protect it with troops. Juárez needed the $2 million granted him by the treaty because his Liberal Party was in the midst of a civil war with the Conservatives. The latter denounced the treaty as a sell-out of the fatherland. That would echo ironically in a few years when Conservatives brought in French armies and Maximilian of Habsburg as "emperor" to shore up a reactionary position they could not protect with their own Mexican resources. The remarkable thing about the McLane-Ocampo Treaty in the eyes of posterity was that Juárez, the supreme Mexican hero, could have so compromised Mexican sovereignty. But the U.S. Senate rejected the treaty, and it merely became, for later Mexicans, an example of the dangers of internal dissension.

In the 1860s the United States supported the Juárez resistance to the French armies and intrusive emperor; but the good will generated soon was smothered by Mexican fear of the U.S. capitalists probing south of the border for concessions, especially for railway construction and mining. Some Mexicans, it is true, were convinced that economic growth could only occur with aid from foreign capital and that above all railways were needed to bind together the resources of a big and mountainous land.

Mexicans agreed that what was happening in the new American Southwest was insulting and dangerous. Anglos there treated Mexicans and Mexican-Americans badly. Many border problems of law and order disturbed relations. Mexico was especially resentful of the American tendency to invade Mexican territory in pursuit of bandits or hostile Indians. Not before about 1880 were these irritants offset by an increase in economic ties between the two countires.*

From the 1880s to 1910 relations became more intimate, during the regime of dictator Porfirio Díaz. He aimed to build quickly railways, mining, industries, and commercial agriculture, with maximum use of foreign investment and expertise, making great concessions to attract such interests. This included not only generous railway construction concessions, but attention to prompt payment on foreign loans as well as vast sales of mineral, agricultural, and grazing lands to foreigners. The effort, though, was not marked by any indication that it aimed at ultimate improvement of the lot of the poor peasants and laborers. It demanded and enforced law and order ("bread or the club"—*pan o palo*). It was celebrated abroad as Mexico's first "civilized" regime, bringer of peace, guarantor of the activities of foreigners. Washington thought that the utopia created south of the border was as sound as the dollar.

Some Mexicans thought otherwise. They saw Díaz as not only a bloody dictator, but as selling off the Mexican patrimony. They saw his system sustained by foreign money and other aid. They knew that Washington cooperated with Díaz by delivering to him exiles he considered dangerous. They knew that Washington (and London and Paris) sustained the regime with approval of its political methods and its petitions to international financiers. So for all the smoothness of certain sorts of high-level financial and political relations between the neighbors during the Díaz dictatorship, it added in most Mexican minds another layer of resentment of the United States.

That resentment was increased by American reaction to the Mexican Revolution of 1910–1917. The revolution destroyed much of the social basis of the Díaz regime along with the

---

*On relations during those years, see chapter 3 and chapter 4.

narrow conservatism that afflicted the country so often after 1821. Americans did not know, or care, about that. The culture south of the border was so different and "inferior" that it scarcely engaged American attention, except on a narrow range of sensational events. In addition, special interests in the United States wished to protect their investments in Mexico, and the Washington government habitually supposed that its views must be given sympathetic consideration there. Finally, Americans had a strong distaste for "revolutions," because their own orderly and successful society had no need for such violence. They could not think of revolutions as necessary or moral; nor could they appreciate that rules for ordinary times could not prevail during such an upheaval.

The Revolution of 1910–1917, and its aftermath until about 1940, quickened old Mexican fears of the United States, especially that it would become more active in intervening in Mexican affairs. At the same time, fears arose in the United States of a radically different Mexican society, not only less subservient to its neighbor but bent on changes that seemed to threaten American property interests and possibly the very bases of Western capitalist society. A cyclone of change and threatened change kept relations between the neighbors badly—at times dangerously—disturbed from 1911 until the beginning of World War II. More than a quarter-century of bad relations left a rich legacy of resentment—especially in Mexico, because those events meant more there than in the United States. And Americans thereafter would have some difficulty appreciating the bitterness of Mexico's recollections of those years.

Radicalism to the United States meant both change of any magnitude and especially socialism or, even worse, communism, which in the 1920s and 1930s often was called bolshevism. Destruction of U.S. property and personal injury to American citizens during a civil war was bad enough, but critics found even more frightening the tendency of the Mexican Revolution to call for changes in the law of property.

Peasants squatting on land around burned-out hacienda houses aroused less sympathy than fright north of the border.

While America feared revolution in Mexico, leaders in that country feared intervention, which was really a refusal by the United States to let Mexico determine its own destiny. Torrents of criticism poured forth from both countries, much of it nearly hysterical with rage or frustration, some icily derogatory, much of it difficult to forget or forgive.

At the beginning of the disturbances, and before anyone could guess what revolutionary wind would sweep Mexico, the United States had as ambassador to Mexico Henry Lane Wilson, who did as much as any diplomat could do to worsen relations with the country to which he was accredited. Without Washington's permission, H. L. Wilson in 1913 plotted the ouster of the recently elected reform President Francisco Madero, and became at least a near accessory to the murder of the gentle Madero by a reactionary group led by General Victoriano Huerta. What did it matter to Mexicans that Wilson acted "independently"? He was the representative of the United States, and it was Washington's responsibility to appoint respectable envoys and to supervise and discipline them. *The Blame of Henry Lane Wilson* became the title of a well-known Mexican book and a phrase that echoed through the decades thereafter.

After Woodrow Wilson's presidential inauguration in March 1913, he replaced H. L. Wilson and then set himself to bring order to a neighbor full of civil war, which had spilled over the common border. Woodrow Wilson was a man of firm intelligence and aims, but unfortunately he had no conception of his own ignorance of Mexican society and persisted in demanding things that it could not or would not perform. Equally unfortunate was the combination of conviction of rectitude and rightness, together with a traditional American patronizing attitude toward Mexico, that prevented Wilson from recognizing his errors. It was also unfortunate that he had less good advice from persons knowledgeable about Mexico than later presidents would have.

Wilson fully justified Mexican fears of intervention. He changed the American requirement for recognition from the neutral basis of de facto control of a country to an emotion-laden and theoretical de jure basis. Wilson thus took upon himself the burden of deciding when a Mexican regime had a "right" to recognition. To Mexicans, not only was that inter-vention an impertinence, but Wilson seemed to define the "purity" of Mexican contestants in a personal way. He never understood that the inflamed nationalism of the leaders of the Revolution meant they would not accept his judgments. What he considered their "stubbornness" was for him forever a mystery. He could not see why his intervention against Huerta was not pleasing to Carranza, who benefited from it but who rejected any United States intrusion into the internal affairs of Mexico.

A trifling incident in 1914 at Tampico, main port of the oil fields, was mishandled by an American admiral stationed off the coast. He wanted demeaning concessions from the Huerta forces. Such minor bumbling could have been smoothed over easily by Washington. Instead, President Wilson acquiesced in the admiral's iniative, and reinforced Mexicans' anger at him by following that acquiescence immediately with the seizure of Veracruz. Mexicans were killed in the invasion. Wilson thought he was justified by a need to bring down the murderer Huerta by blocking arms imports and customs receipts.

During those years, American oil and mining companies, landowners in Mexico, and conservatives generally decried the "mild" policy of Wilson. That was known, of course, in Mexico. A State Department officer suggested an American-supported counterrevolution in Mexico. Although rejected by President Wilson, it was known and condemned by Mexican nationalists and served to entice a defeated Pancho Villa into adventures—including raids into the United States—that would prove his anti-American position. Wilson even for a time was enamored of the supposed virtues of the mercurial and primitive Villa.

The fury against the United States in Mexico even encouraged Germany during World War I to speculate on the possibility of a connection there. The German consul in Tampico hatched some fanciful schemes. For example, the German foreign office in the famous "Zimmermann telegram of 1917" tried a feeler to Carranza that included reference to the "lost territories" in the southwestern United States. Revelation of that in the United States increased distaste for the Kaiser's Germany, though it did not necessarily alert Americans to the possible dangers of a hostile Mexico next door. Most people did not take Mexico seriously—an attitude Mexicans did not find endearing.

Relations remained roiled in the 1920s and 1930s by problems of recognition, claims for damages, disputes over the new system of land expropriations, and new regulations on oil drilling and ownership. Although for awhile the United States used nonrecognition as a weapon against President Alvaro Obregón (1920–1924), it dropped that method thereafter, partly because of a general United States disillusion with nonrecognition and intervention. The forays between 1895 and 1933 into the affairs of Venezuela, Cuba, Santo Domingo, Nicaragua, Mexico, and Haiti produced little more than Latin American resentment. So in 1933 the new administration of Franklin D. Roosevelt proclaimed the "Good Neighbor" policy and agreed with the Western Hemisphere nations in the Pan American Union to abandon intervention. That ditching of a failed policy was emphasized in 1938 when Roosevelt declined to intervene following Mexico's expropriation of foreign oil properties. Mexico thus became a pioneer in the successful resistance by what later would be called the Third World to the tutelage of the industrial powers.

In addition to American fears of Mexican "bolshevism"

during and after the Revolution, there were cries against Mexico's supposed "atheism." American Roman Catholics were unable to understand antichurch actions as "anticlerical" rather than "antireligious," which was natural enough since anticlericalism had no reason for existence in an America of religious pluralism and consensus against an established church. Nor did the public schools acquaint citizens with the great struggles over established religion in the Catholic countries of Europe and Latin America, where anticlericalism was an important phenomenon. The Catholic parochial schools also preferred to ignore the fact that good Catholics in many countries had insisted that the church's property and political habits be reformed.

American Catholic complaints swelled. Fortunately, the administrations in Washington never considered intervention for that reason. Many Americans either were indifferent to the issue or even rather sympathetic with the official Mexican position. That did not, however, reconcile Mexicans in the face of a clamor for intervention raised by American Catholic organizations and ecclesiastics north of the border.

All church property was expropriated by the Mexican state, which proposed to keep the temples open itself, permitting the church to use them. Churchmen were forbidden to express political opinions, priests were required to register with the government, and the states of the Mexican federal union were permitted to regulate the number of priests within their territories. On one occasion a Mexican state found one priest to be sufficient! Serious outrages against churchmen, nuns, and the sanctity of temples occurred during the Revolution.

Although such conditions were not acceptable to the hierarchy in Mexico, or to the Vatican, apparently most Mexicans accepted them or were indifferent. A considerable minority of laymen supported the church, in part because it was a way of objecting to all the innovations of the Revolution. Tensions came to crisis stage in 1926 when the primate of Mexico spoke out (not for the first time) against the new rules, and President Plutarco Calles took punitive measures against what he considered defiance of the constitutional system. The church then declared an interdict against the performance of priestly functions, an ancient but now anachronistic church weapon. A pro-church, and antiadministration, faction in central Mexico took up arms in the Cristero Rebellion (1926–29). After atrocities committed by both sides, the rebellion was crushed. Thereafter, happily, some U.S. Catholics helped arrange a compromise between the Mexican government and the hierarchy in Mexico and the Vatican.

So United States–Mexican relations gradually were stabilized, concessions being made by both sides. Not only were the issues more or less resolved, but United States involvement in World War II and Mexican involvement in great economic growth, occasioned in part by the war, made remaining differences diminish in importance.*

From World War II to the early 1970s relations between the neighbors generally were much less abrasive. Damage claims, oil rights, land division, most boundary questions, and many other matters had been reasonably well settled. When they required adjustment, that usually was done without too much trouble. Mexico was busy with economic development; the United States was busy with new global tasks and was pleased with stable political conditions in Mexico, with the reduction of tensions, and with the fact that Mexico did not use the Cold War against the United States.

The worst problems were Mexican nationalist fears of American economic domination, distaste for U.S. interventions against supposed communist threats in several Latin American countries, Mexican irritation that the United States would not buy more Mexican goods, and American uneasi-

---

*See chapter 3 on the Mexican Revolution; chapter 4 on post-Revolution nationalism in Mexico; chapter 5 on the Mexican experience with foreign oil investors and the expropriation of 1938.

ness at illegal Mexican immigration to the north. Clashes over these matters generally were not bitter until the arrival of the administration of Luis Echeverría (1970–1976). He embittered relations by escalating Mexican demands for economic aid and then by assuming leadership of Third World insistence on redistribution of wealth. His successor, José López Portillo, continued the sharp criticism of American policies, either out of conviction or to appear as nationalistic as Echeverría, or because he considered that to be the best way to gain concessions. His strictures coincided with great new Mexican oil production, upon which the United States hoped to draw, and with an escalation of United States fears of uncontrolled illegal immigration, much of it from Mexico. The last year of the 1970s thus saw less cordiality between the neighbors, and the 1980s promised to be less easy than the 1950s and 1960s.

How much does recollection of past events affect current Mexico–United States relations? More than for most countries, because Mexico remembers so vividly much that it dislikes. The history of asserted infamies and slights by the United States is constantly under review. Mexico not only asks, as do we all, what have you done for me recently? It also is not just content to remind us of what we did to it recently, but has a ready list of complaints stretching back for more than a century.

Diplomatic Goals and Methods

A remarkable military policy defines the Mexican international stance: maintenance of only small and cheap armed forces. Some 85,000 military personnel suffice for a nation of 65 million, and the cost is less than five percent of the national budget, a great blessing to Mexico's economic and social programs. It means that Mexico considers it useless to arm against the United States, pointless to plan adventures in nearby weak countries, and that it counts on American protection from marauding world powers.

Mexico seldom takes action that involves serious economic sacrifices merely out of ideological or emotional reasons. It wishes for the maximum possible freedom in international relations, meaning, especially, deviation from United States lines on such inexpensive matters as recognition of nonconstitutional regimes, and a benign attitude toward what Mexico considers "reform" or "clean revolutionary" governments. It does recognize the difficulty of reducing much its economic dependence on the United States and the dangers of departing too vividly from the global political views of Washington.

Other major foreign policy goals include improvement of the economy by increasing economic exchange, avoidance of American reprisals (especially deportations) against Mexicans illegally north of the border, and no great extensions of United States border restrictions or guard methods. Mexico promotes by international agreement the ideas of nonintervention and the juridical equality of states as well as support of such agencies as the United Nations and the Organization of American States, which favor these ideas. It strongly supports the nineteenth-century Argentine Calvo Doctrine, requiring that foreign-owned property receive only the protection accorded the property of nationals, thus rejecting diplomatic pressure. Mexico also insists on its own Estrada Doctrine of 1930, calling for the immediate recognition of de facto governments, thus dismissing as irrelevant the political coloration of the new regime or the manner in which it came to power. That is a declaration that the punitive use of recognition is unacceptable, being intervention and interference with sovereignty. Mexico has not quite been able to live up to this ideal.

Finally, we may take it that Mexican leaders long to see their country play a much greater role in global affairs, but they do not say so; always realistic, they recognize how far Mexico is from such a role and that discussion of it now probably would be politically counterproductive.

Mexican methods used in pursuit of its goals differ from

those of the United States because Mexico is a weak country dealing with a superpower, because America has worldwide strategic goals and Mexico's interest is fastened on a narrower range of goals, and because Mexican institutions are much different from those of the United States.

The Mexican executive is somewhat less constrained than the American by political considerations. The "one party dominant" political system subjects the president to pressures from factions within the PRI (Institutional Revolutionary Party), but no other party threatens to win elections should a serious error be made. The Mexican congress is nearly a nullity, and exercises almost no constraint on the president. Organized interest groups are less important in Mexico than they are in America because of the one-party system, the subservient congress, and weaker state governments. Organized labor is a part of the PRI, with little independent voice in international affairs. Organized business has less influence than in the United States, because it is not part of the PRI, can find no effective help from the minority parties, can accomplish little by lobbying federal or state legislatures, and has less influence with the public than business has in the United States. The intellectual elite often decry the government line on foreign relations, but they are few and unorganized. They also lack influence because poor education and lack of political sophistication and activism among the population leaves intellectuals with but a small audience. Furthermore, the press in Mexico, though it prints much criticism of official foreign policy, is sufficiently influenced by government to proceed with some caution.

The methods of diplomacy available to Mexico in dealing with the United States are limited. Mexico can vote against American positions in the United Nations, but that is of little value. In general, the United States will "pay" little for support in the U.N., because the U.N. is not very important in world affairs and because the United States has the veto power. Mexico was reminded of its vulnerability when in 1975 it voted for a U.N. resolution equating Zionism with racism; American Jews punished Mexico by boycotting the latter's tourist attractions, to the tune of possibly $200 million in the next year.

Mexico might use control of illegal immigration as a counter, but it does not want to control it, and it would take a large American quid pro quo to change the Mexican attitude on the "safety valve." Also, Mexico can extract a price on relatively minor issues where it does not seem expedient to Washington to exert much power: e.g., water division and salinity, fishing rights, or minor boundary adjustments. Mexico, furthermore, can exert only modest pressure on American investment because Mexico wants more, if not in the older lines then in newer ones, or under new conditions.

So Mexico oscillates between soft words and aggressive demands, partly in response to domestic political imperatives, partly out of frustration. Echeverría's abrasiveness during the years 1970–76 did not serve the country well, so López Portillo began with softer tones—although his remarks in a personal appearance before the U.S. Congress in February 1977 contained some barbs. When sweet reason got him little but criticism at home, López Portillo turned on harsher tones. That tactic of frigidity and rhetorical harshness was displayed during the February 1979 visit to Mexico of President Jimmy Carter. López Portillo was correct but deliberately stiff, and he lectured the American president on the shortcomings of his country's policy. Carter tried to reply amiably and slipped in a feeble pun on "Montezuma's revenge," the diarrhea so many tourists contract in Mexico. When actors compete, good writers are useful. As the *New York Times* explained, "It is hard to defend a president who begins a goodwill mission . . . by reminiscing about" diarrhea, and that "stylistically the Carter administration's foreign relations seem to have lost all sense of class." That was, of course, "Grandma

Times" at her most pontifical, and one would have thought that style and class as measures of policy would have gone out after President John Kennedy's admirers so mushily abused the idea.

The United States often thinks that it endures a superfluity of certain staples of Mexican rhetoric: a flamboyant anti-interventionism that often seems unrelated to reality; a "liberalism" on international issues that makes headlines and also makes the United States seem reactionary, often unfairly, and seldom affects fundamental Mexican policy; a Latin American and Mexican nationalism that often seems anti-Yanqui, and sometimes anticapitalist, though Mexican policies scarcely support either of those ideas.

Intelligent leaders on both sides, of course, can see the hollowness of the rhetoric and posing in both countries. But some leaders are not intelligent, and others have different fish to fry, including the making of political mileage when no other gains seem available. López Portillo's words are sustained, of course, by the fact that Mexico's new oil and natural gas resources permit it to be more aggressive. It has judged—probably correctly—that the United States eventually would pay premium prices and possibly make concessions on other economic matters, rather than attempt drastic pressures on Mexico. Some Americans suspected that this was the case partly because the discipline required for other decisions was not present in the United States; other Americans, that it simply was not worth other methods; yet others, that the quality of recent Mexican chief executives might be higher than those north of the border.

American goals as they affect Mexico include (1) a friendly, stable nation along its southern border; (2) Mexican support internationally—or at least a minimum of difference—on vital issues; (3) aid in monitoring persons in Mexico thought to be a threat to the United States; (4) help in fighting the export smuggling of narcotics and marijuana across the border; (5)

cooperation in regulating, possibly even damming, the flow of Mexicans to the U.S.; and (6) a favorable climate for American private investment in Mexico.

The methods used by the United States in its relations with Mexico may be described as aiming at maximization of profit (not just monetary) under clouds of camouflage; in short, they usually have been conservative and highly rational. The camouflage was not intended so much for Mexican statesmen, although it occasionally helped save face for the latter, but for the American public, so practical in many ways, but often misled by nonessentials in foreign affairs. No doubt that was partly because of concern for world affairs in a dangerous age, and partly a lack of access to all the mysteries; but also it was due to a curious belief that haggling over world affairs could be made less sordid than haggling over sales of rugs and peanuts.

Mexican statesmen understandably found American methods irritating; American statesmen/politicians naturally continued methods that seemed to serve them well. It was, of course, foolish to criticize American procedures as hypocritical, since indirection is part of the definition of diplomacy. Nor was the frequent charge of lack of imagination impressive; the United States merely took advantage of its power. It scarcely was unique in that, and it was obvious that Mexican —and other foreign—statesmen despised Washington when it seemed to forget that power. A few intellectuals thought it worthwhile to urge that it was psychologically easier for the strong than for the weak to make concessions, but that was a half-truth—possibly a tenth-truth—better left in the closet.

A favorite Washington device is sloganeering, in which a "great new initiative," usually with a catchy name, is announced as a result of an inexpensive brain-storming session. Although the United States has no patent on that method, it is quite good at it, yet it has overestimated its value. Latin Americans certainly considered they had a surfeit of Good Neighbor policies, Alliances for Progress, and the like. A recent example was the brainchild of Henry Kissinger, who as secretary of state talked of a "New Dialogue" with Latin America to create better understanding. Latin America quickly showed plenty of understanding (which Kissinger no doubt knew from the beginning), so he dropped the New Dialogue when it had served its unannounced ephemeral purpose. Mexico has no trouble equating sloganeering with empty promises.

Sloganeering is sensible, however, because it is cheap, as long as practitioners are not bemused by their own rhetoric. That is the danger; it was linked to the dream of cheap solutions. More bangs for a buck. Fire the manager! Old Potawattomy Snake Oil for curvature of the spine.

Another cosmetic tactic dedicated to the cheap solution is the "good will" or "fact finding" mission. They usually were used without hope of accomplishing more than a relaxation of criticism, at home or abroad. Kissinger, just after becoming secretary of state in 1973, hurried to Mexico to assure President Echeverría that Washington "still" thought it a special partner. Mexico managed to restrain its enthusiasm. Unhappily, some United States officials, even presidents, occasionally believed that their charming and intelligent presence abroad would smooth out issues resistant to ironing. Even when the poor things had little hope of that, they often felt compelled to go in the very different hope that a "success," or even a pleasant greeting, would elevate their support in the polls at home. Recently, it has sometimes been difficult to arrange a really pleasant greeting in Mexico. If that were to reduce cosmetic tours designed to "save" foreign relations, it might be a sanitary thing for all concerned.

The search for cheap solutions often has a valid point, but a mangled one. A favorite recommendation is for more "imagination" in foreign relations, almost as though Merlin or Shakespeare could blow away hard realities. New and better-coordinated study and policy structures constantly are urged; but often the recommendations are vague and naive, and usually exaggerate the importance of such action.

In late 1978 and early 1979 the press favorably reported that the administration was considering closer coordination between federal departments dealing with Mexico, so that such issues as energy, immigration, and trade could be tackled as a single interrelated "package." Packaging is popular in America. The *Washington Post* in February 1979 declared that issues with Mexico "can no longer be handed over to lieutenants for narrow solutions, as the Mexican gas issue has been handled"—as though President Carter or Saint Peter could make Mexico prefer lower prices for natural gas. The *Post* in April 1979 was sympathetic to the idea of a special interagency coordinator for Mexican-American affairs, but wisely described it as "experimental." In the same month it opposed the notion of a Mexican-American as ambassador to Mexico, declaring that such offices should not be the preserve of ethnic minorities.

Education, another commonly presented solution to international problems, is not cheap and is probably as unrealistic as coordinators and presidential smiles. The role of education and better understanding is the conventional wisdom in some news media, church, civil libertarian, and academic circles. The kernel of truth in this idea, however, is outweighed by its misleading implications. Surely, education and understanding could sometimes be valuable to the promotion of international harmony. On the other hand, they sometimes induce distaste rather than cooing agreement.

Possibly the most useful educational effort would be to reduce demagoguery in both Mexico and the United States. That being chimerical, other sorts of institutions do what they can. Latin American programs at United States universities lead the way in foreign area studies, chronologically and in terms of size, by providing experts for further teaching, government service, and advice to private enterprise. It does not noticeably reduce tensions between the neighbors, though. Nor does extensive tourism by both sides, any more than it determines foreign relations between France and Italy. The

great influx of Mexicans here has affected American culture
—for example, restaurants and even markets—but that matters no more to foreign relations than did the great and delightful invasion of Italian food some years earlier.

Mexicans ate at such Anglo chain outlets south of the
border as Denny's, Aunt Jemima's, Burger King, and Kentucky Fried Chicken—all with possible damage to their diges-
tion as well as esthetic standards, but there has been no ob-
servable effect on grand affairs. American movies and television programs abound in Mexico, with the same ambiguous
effects on morals and manners as they have on those north of
the border—and none on affairs of state. The Ballet Folk-
lórico de México delights North Americans, without improving their understanding of natural gas pricing. The Rockefeller
Foundation in Mexico does marvelous work in promoting the
Green Revolution, but it is a matter of, What have you done
for me recently?

It has been nearly half a century since the Rockefellers
ripped Diego Rivera's leftist murals from the walls of their
music hall, with no discernible effect today. Also, half a
century has gone by since Dartmouth College, no center of
leftism, paid José Clemente Orozco to paint a number of
square yards of its library basement with vivid condemnations
of capitalism. No stream of communists has issued from the
New Hampshire hills, nor do Dartmouth alumni hate or love
Mexico more than those of Yale do.

Generally Routine Issues

Some issues between the neighbors in recent years generally
have been handled with a minimum of trouble. Occasionally
there is a flareup, but usually it dies down, either because
there is a compromise between parties or because public
interest is tepid.

1. Allocation of television channels is necessary for neighbors, and is done fairly easily, because the short range trans-

mission causes a minimum of interference. Radio is more difficult. The United States wants what its radio industry can afford—that is, a blanket over the Mexican market; and Mexico wants to protect itself. Adjustments are needed periodically.

2. Most disputes over the location of the boundary involve little but punctilio. The shifting bed of the Rio Grande has long caused problems. Agreements have failed to solve all issues until recently. For example, an area known as the "Chamizal" in the El Paso, Texas, area was the most notorious little bone of contention. International arbitration early in the twentieth century divided the territory, but Washington refused to accept it. At last, in 1963, the two countries agreed to divide a few acres of land, set out to confine the Rio Grande to unshiftable channels, and agreed to solve all other boundary problems.

3. Negotiation of reciprocal air transport rights occasions sharp disputes without inflaming national passions. Mexico, developing its own airlines, has demanded that American lines be restricted. Essentially, American carriers favor "free competition," while Mexicans cannot compete. When Mexico began granting concessions to third country airlines, the United States had to pay more attention. So there was compromise on routes, frequency of service, and other matters. Adjustments occasionally are necessary.

4. Pollution wafting across the border has caused some dispute. A lead smelter in El Paso, for example, permitted emissions that reportedly caused lead poisoning in some 10,000 children in both countries. An investigation in 1977 indicated that the threat was especially great to Mexican children directly across the Rio Grande from the smelter. The company began installing scrubbing equipment, on orders from a court and after the Mexican government took an interest in the matter.

5. There are problems of violence along the border, inevitable when certain cities there are so large and when there is so much movement of people back and forth, and so much

difference between economic levels in the two countries. Swarms of illegal immigrants moving from the Tijuana area toward nearby San Diego and Los Angeles are preyed on by Mexican gangs and draw gunfire from the police of both countries. The police also sometimes fire at each other. Some Mexican police collaborate with Mexican "coyotes," smugglers of men north across the border, some of that Mexican police activity taking place in United States territory. Officials of San Diego and Tijuana met in 1977 to try to deal with their problems. The mayor of San Diego also appealed directly to the presidents of the two countries for help in dealing with an "interstate problem" of violence. It is bound to be a continuing sore spot.

6. There is cooperation in the control of several animal disorders, including hoof-and-mouth disease. The United States for a long time paid for the slaughter of infected cattle in Mexico, then when Mexican cattlemen created too much pressure on their government, a switch was made to vaccination.

7. There are a great variety of lawsuits involving private citizens of both countries, sometimes involving government. Most of the suits achieve only minor notice. Sometimes they fail when they try to get a national court to adjudicate a matter that lies in the jurisdiction of the other country.

8. There still are claims arising out of the Treaty of 1848. Reies López Tijerina, the Mexican-American leader from New Mexico, would prefer to get the disputed land rather than monetary reparations, but in 1977 he conceded that the former would be difficult to arrange after so many years. Most claimants have been willing to take money. In 1923 Mexico and the United States agreed to adjustment of claims arising from the old border settlement. Each was to reimburse its own citizens. The United States did so, but Mexico has not reimbursed the American claimants who are the heirs of the Old Mexican and Spanish holders of the pre-1848 period.

9. The Pious Fund of the Californias was established in

the seventeenth century in Mexico to foster Catholic missionary activity in the Californias. The Jesuits were in charge, and when they were ousted from the Spanish dominions in 1767, Spain, then later Mexico, took over the fund. There was argument as to what to do when Upper California became part of the United States. Mexico paid some money irregularly into the fund but stopped with the Revolution of 1910. Mexico in 1967 agreed to pay a lump sum of under $1 million to an endowment for a seminary in New Mexico to educate priests for duty in Mexico. The seminary closed in 1972 and the endowment was transferred to the Mexican church hierarchy.

10. A little-noticed dispute has worsened recently over illegal removal from Mexico of archaeological treasures. It is difficult to control because many of the sites are in remote locations. Citizens of both countries are willing to steal the treasures, even to use power saws to rip off the inscriptions on ancient Maya stelae in Yucatan. Rich collectors—individual and institutional—abroad, including the United States, are willing to buy.

11. Occasionally an American suggests that a canal across the Mexican Isthmus of Tehuantepec would be useful, and that possibly it might be excavated with nuclear explosives. The U.S. State Department does not pursue the matter.

12. The drug problem at the border will remain, probably unsolvable and oscillating in and out of public notice.

13. Few Americans have been much interested in disputes over the definition of territorial waters. The old three-mile limit has been breaking up, and in the 1930s and 1940s Mexico and the United States modestly increased jurisdiction beyond that. In the 1950s Mexico acted against United States fishing boats inside its nine-mile claim. There were American objections, but it was a worldwide problem. Peru and Ecuador claimed control of fishing rights out to two hundred miles from their shores. The United States gradually yielded and adopted the two hundred mile control of fishing itself, being as much concerned with Soviet and Japanese fishing near its

coasts as Mexico with San Diego boats in Mexican waters. Delimitation of zones is proceeding.

14. Other border concerns cause flurries of interest. Such issues include short border fences in critical areas, meticulous rather than routine searches of persons and vehicles, much of the seizure of contraband and the treatment of the culprits, changes in procedures with regard to tourist and commuter cards.

15. The 1944 water treaty required the United States to send into Mexico in the Colorado River 1.5 million acre-feet annually of water of agricultural quality (not too salty). This became difficult as the great postwar growth of population in the Southwest put pressure on water supplies. It was especially troublesome in Arizona and California. Various recent projects tapped the river, for example, the Parker Dam about 150 miles south of Hoover Dam; and the huge Colorado Aqueduct that ran through desert and mountains some 250 miles from the river to the Los Angeles area reduced water supplies further. More Colorado River water also was carried to the Imperial and Coachella Valleys of California, which by the 1970s had thousands of miles of irrigation channels and grew more than two crops a year, worth over half a billion dollars. The valleys annually used nearly twice as much Colorado River water as the United States delivered to Mexico.

The Glen Canyon Dam in northern Arizona began in 1963 to create Lake Powell, storing nearly a two-year supply at the "natural and average" rate of the river's flow. But drought in 1976–1977 made new supplies less than average and nothing about demand was "natural." Meanwhile, Phoenix and Tucson grew like weeds, watered by wells into deep aquifers containing ancient water. That drove down the water table, so that future growth was threatened. Arizona then drew big plans for the use of Colorado River water. Mexico would liked to have made such plans. Both California and Arizona also dreamed of bringing water from the Columbia River, Canada, or even Alaska. They snarled at eastern suggestions that less growth of population, agriculture, and industry also was a solution.

By 1960 the Colorado River water reaching Mexico had far too much salt—resulting from irrigation use—and was reducing the productivity of Mexican farms. Mexico repeatedly protested. The United States spent millions between 1961 and 1972 trying to better the water. It was not enough. In the early 1970s President Echeverría declared that the salinity of Colorado River water was the major issue between the two countries. That was an exaggeration, but it illustrated the way an originally small dispute could grow.

Mexico was not entirely without power of retaliation. It pumped ground water just south of the border so as to tap supplies in the United States. The latter did "protective pumping" in counter-retaliation. Finally, in 1972 then-President Nixon agreed to large-scale desalinization of Colorado River water, and the Colorado River Basin Salinity Act was passed in 1974.

The first plant—the world's largest—was constructed at Yuma, Arizona. Initial talk was of a $100-million investment by federal taxpayers; then the figure rose until by 1977 it was an estimated $316 million for the Yuma plant and associated facilities. Great amounts of energy were required for the desalinization process. Probably the cost figures would go up further. Even more dismaying, the Yuma effort might deliver to Mexico only a tenth of the guaranteed 1.5 million acre-feet of agricultural quality water. The final bill on compliance with United States obligations to Mexico for Colorado River water ultimately would run into the billions, with large costs continuing in perpetuity.

Nor is that necessarily all. Mexico might become dissatisfied with the 1.5 million acre-feet agreement. Its rapidly increasing population has made more agricultural production essential. How could the United States answer a request for adjustment of the agreement? A flat "no" scarcely would be acceptable, especially since Mexico has supplies of natural gas and oil much desired in the United States. Furthermore, Mexico could again increase use of water in its rivers feeding into the lower Rio Grande, which again would bring pressure on Washington from Texans.

There are other contestants for the waters of the Southwest: five Indian groups in Arizona. They have carried many water-rights cases to the courts, where they were resisted by the Anglo farmers in the valley of the Gila river, a tributary of the Colorado. The Indians even persuaded Senator Edward Kennedy of faraway Massachusetts to introduce a bill guaranteeing Indians a share of water. That inevitably would reduce water for Anglo farmers.

United States and Mexican officials constantly check the Colorado for salinity and volume of flow. Americans release not a drop more than necessary. Mexico's Morelos Dam stops what crosses the border; beyond the dam, the Colorado is a creek. All this is of absorbing interest in the far Southwest, but, as that region is angrily aware, not considered very important by well-watered states.

Major Political Issues

An issue may have both political and economic aspects, so that categorization merely shows its predominant character. Chiefly political issues are more intractable than economic ones. For example, it is easier to imagine a profound Mexican concession on economic exchange than on intervention in Mexican affairs. Of course, an economic demand can be perceived as intervention, in which case political emotions wash it with angry hues.

American Gentleness with Mexico

Washington is notably careful not to even appear to interfere in Mexican affairs. It is too pleased with Mexico's current political stability and economic growth to risk offending its prickly neighbor. Washington praises Mexico's "preferred revolution," an alternative to Castro and proof that the United States is not against all change in Latin America. How much this muffling of criticism is worth to Mexico in concrete terms is arguable. Some Americans think it has gone far enough. The *New York Times* in February 1979 referred to a "cocky" Mexico. It also reported that the press there complained that the United States tried to buy natural gas at cut-rate prices; but the papers did not bother to point out that Mexico's asking price was higher than Canada's. The director of PEMEX said that poor communications with Washington left the American position unclear. That was an old ploy. Washington's position was clear enough; what was uncertain, as the PEMEX director knew, was whether the U.S. government would stick to it.

Washington's gentle ways with Mexico have met attack from those Americans who say that the neighbor is a dictatorship and violated human rights. With the growth of the civil libertarian movement, that charge has put some minor pressure on Washington. In February 1979 the Council on Hemisphere Affairs, a combination of labor, civil rights, education, and church elements, accused the Mexican government of political repression and inhuman treatment of political dissenters, and it said that Washington's oil policy made it reluctant to offend Mexico. At issue were supposedly "missing prisoners" of the Mexican government, their treatment, and the question of which Mexicans deserved political asylum in the United States. A California congressman said that one refugee spoke for human rights against a government "using institutionalized terror and violence masquerading as law."

The same month the Mexican government, responding to pressure by such groups as Amnesty International, announced the results of an investigation into 314 supposed cases of disappearance, finding 154 dead as rural guerrillas, 98 still operating as guerrillas, and 62 accounted for in a variety of ways. It also said there were no secret jails in Mexico, no torture, and no special anti-guerrilla forces surreptitiously committing atrocities. Of course, critics—including the mothers of missing sons—did not accept the report.

It is a vexatious matter because it is both complex and subject to various interpretations, depending on point of view and degree of knowledge. A minority of American opinion-makers and scholars long has been critical of Mexican society. It claims that that view is dictated by "liberalism." It is not much interested in the naive view that American reluctance to offend Mexico is due simply to oil policy. Long before Mexico offered large oil exports, those critics objected to what they thought was official American unwillingness to describe Mexican conditions objectively. For those critics, there are evils south of the border that require much more attention along the Potomac.

A larger body of American opinion, however, rejects that criticism as exaggerated and as deliberately isolating Mexican institutions rather than comparing them with other areas of the world more deserving of the displeasure of liberals. Those of this view agree that Mexico is different from the United States but insist that it also is quite different from Uganda or the Soviet Union. They furthermore insist that the Mexican political and social system is one of the freer and more benign in the world, coming immediately after twenty-one more open societies—fifteen in noncommunist Europe, plus the United States, Canada, Australia, New Zealand, Japan, and Costa Rica.

Forms of Mexican Nationalism

This not-very-vigorous debate in the United States has not reduced the Mexican fear of American domination that was at the core of its foreign policy, just as it remains an important ingredient in Mexico's domestic politics. To Mexicans, being neighbor to the United States is akin to living next to a "reformed" burglar: remembrance of past actions prompting paranoia about locking the windows. Fear of political dictation, on either domestic or international issues, is reinforced by fear of economic domination, or of cultural or spiritual pulverization by the colossus of the north.

These nationalist terrors make a mighty engine for the mobilization of Mexican opinion. The Mexican national spirit is so potent and volatile that the government and national party cannot entirely control it. Even Coca-Cola signs provoke growls of distaste at the subtle and sinister threat of Yanqui imperialism. Critics of the regime rouse Mexicanidad, and the establishment must respond, willy-nilly. Nationalism is a slippery tiger to ride.

One form that the distaste for United States tutelage takes is complaint that Washington disdains Mexico by neglecting its views and its needs, especially as compared with other countries. The latter part of this refers to the huge rehabilitation aid provided Europe and Asia after World War II, as well as the obvious concentration of United States attention in recent years on the Old World. Mexican leaders know, but are not interested in, the strong reasons for those American policies. They simply say they are not treated as an equal. López Portillo was reported in October 1978 as saying that "Mexico is neither on the list of United States priorities nor on that of United States respect." The *Washington Post* in a February 1979 editorial supported that view in milder terms by noting that in the United States the "Mexican Connection" —not a happy phrase to use—only recently was seen as requiring direct and sustained attention.

Another form that Mexican nationalism takes is insistence on at least appearing to have an independent foreign policy. Opposition to the wars in Korea and Vietnam was a way of showing that, although they also were objected to as being interference in the affairs of other nations. An independent foreign policy, together with the hope of profit, no doubt was mingled in with President Echeverría's promotion through the U.N. in December 1974 of the Charter of Economic Rights and Duties, which called on the industrialized powers to share the wealth with the Third World. Leadership of the Third

World, so assiduously pursued by Echeverría, partly served the desire for an independent foreign policy, although Echeverría also wanted to be U.N. secretary general. An independent foreign policy was one reason for Mexican support of Panama's demand for return of the Panama Canal Zone. And it was part of Mexico's promotion of the Treaty of Tlateloclo against nuclear proliferation in the Western Hemisphere, although certainly Mexico also hoped the treaty would give protection. It certainly would not prevent nuclear proliferation, as Brazil's determined pursuit of nuclear power, and probably weapons, indicated.

Disagreements over Communism and Violence

Disagreement between the neighbors over communism has taken many forms, often involved Mexican nationalism, its belief that its advice and needs were neglected by the United States, and the desire for an independent Mexican foreign policy. The series of United States interventions in Latin America to meet perceived communist threats after World War II provoked many of those disagreements. Mexico objected to American intervention of any sort in the Western Hemisphere, as a violation of the nonintervention pledges given since 1933. Mexico has taken the view that any intervention threatens every country unable to match Washington's military power. Mexico incidentally doubts the seriousness of threats of communist subversion in the Western Hemisphere, or that the United States could not meet them when they became more clearly manifest. In effect, it has declared that Mexico would inform Washington when there is sufficient threat to justify intervention.

In 1954, the United States supported an intervention by Guatemalan exiles against the Jacobo Arbenz regime, which had accepted communist collaboration. Mexico, and most of Latin America, never accepted the legality of the intervention or the reality of the threat it was supposed to meet. In fact, Latin America argued that United States economic assistance

to the hemispheric nations was more important than communist threats. Some Americans found that argument baffling.

Mexico has disagreed with American policy regarding Fidel
Castro's Cuba on all but one occasion, taking the view that
Cuba was entitled to a revolutionary government if it wanted
it; nor was Mexico interested in suggestions that no one knew
what Cubans wanted under a communist police state. Mexico
constantly has opposed the measures of the Organization of
American States (OAS), usually initiated by the United
States, to condemn or punish Cuba, even when it interfered
in other Latin American countries in attempts to bring down
governments and promote revolution. Mexico condemned the
U.S.-supported effort to use Cuban exiles to bring down
Castro at the Bay of Pigs in 1961. When all the other OAS
nations cut diplomatic relations with Cuba, Mexico refused
to do so. Of course, Canada and the European powers also
maintained relations with Cuba. Mexico also led a campaign
to return Cuba to a full and equal place in the OAS. It disagreed with Washington's objections to Cuban expropriations
of foreign-owned property, remembering similar events in
Mexico's past. It pointed out that during a revolution a government had neither the time nor the money to meet external
demands. Mexico refused to get excited about communist
doctrine and methods in Cuba, confident of its ability to control Mexican communists.

The United States government accepted all of this Mexican
disagreement with little public complaint, partly because Mexico in one crisis joined the rest of the hemisphere in standing
with the United States against Castro's acceptance of Soviet
offensive missiles in 1962. In addition, Washington understood
the political value to the Mexican government and party of the
independent Cuban policy. Finally, strong objections from
Washington would be counterproductive.

Some Americans became permanently disillusioned with
Mexican foreign policy in the 1950s and 1960s. They would
not accept the lack of Mexican sympathy with the U.N. police

action against communist North Korean and Chinese aggression against South Korea. And it seemed to them nearly insane that Mexico would not take strong action against Cuban efforts to revolutionize various countries of the Western Hemisphere. Apparently Mexico was against intervention even to prevent intervention. It seemed to those critics that Mexico was so removed from responsibility for its acts in international affairs that it was able to act with total disregard for realities. After all, the armed forces of the United States, it was said, would protect it from real harm.

Mexico refused to approve the United States invasion of the Dominican Republic in 1965 to defeat a perceived communist threat. Not only did Mexico—and many other Latin American countries—see no threat, but it condemned intervention as contrary to the OAS Charter, as indeed it was. Washington merely thought that there were things more important than the OAS Charter, a view that Mexican purists regarded with horror. Mexico introduced a resolution to the OAS Council calling for withdrawal of American troops from the Dominican Republic. The United States managed to convert the military intervention into a multilateral force under OAS aegis, but much of the organization, including Mexico, opposed that, too. OAS and U.N. pressure forced the withdrawal of the hemispheric troops at the end of 1965.

Mexico opposed United States intervention in Chilean affairs during 1970–1973, and welcomed Chilean exiles from the military coup d'etat of 1973. Mexico even abandoned in this instance its supposedly sacrosanct policy of recognizing de facto governments, refusing to accept the regime of General Augusto Pinochet. It was impossible to know the mix of factors that led Mexican leaders to that decision. Certainly, however, they knew that opposition to suspected United States intervention was popular at home and would scarcely hurt abroad. The extent of their interest in conditions in Chile, or in the amount of American intervention there, was also hard to know. By this time, American opinion was divided between those who found Mexican foreign policy impeccably liberal at every turn and those who found that it required a good deal of patient understanding.

Numerous disagreements between the neighbors over communism were based on different domestic political considerations, readings of global affairs, attitudes toward communism, and responsibilities in world affairs. Mexico asserted that not only did Washington exaggerate the danger of communist subversion, but that in any event Latin Americans should be left to handle it themselves. Indeed, Mexico controlled its own communists with an iron hand. Also, it helped American agents watch who flew to Cuba and what Soviet Bloc personnel were doing in Mexico.

Where did Mexico stand? Some haters of Marx mistakenly thought that communal land holdings such as the big Mexican "ejidos" could only be communist. Others thought that the large public sector of the medical profession in Mexico showed a terrible drift to the left. Many thought that leftist rhetoric spouted by Mexican officials and intellectuals always was to be taken at face value, when they knew better with regard to American public figures. Exaggerated reports of President Echeverría's radicalism led a group of U.S. congressmen to write to President Gerald Ford in 1976 that Mexico was being prepared for a communist takeover. Although the State Department was not fond of Echeverría, it dismissed this effusion as irrational and ignorant.

Congressional and general public difficulties in interpreting Mexican events were no greater than doing it with India or Turkey, but they were far away. Much of it was merely due to reliance on the media rather than spending time and effort on real study. The American media had trouble all over the world in dealing with the phenomena of violence. They often exaggerated its incidence and seldom properly indicated its persistence in societies and the near-impossibility of reducing it with prayers, editorials, and bylined articles. They also fastened on selected violent actions, which became almost media fads; they beat them to death while ignoring others which sometimes involved worse cruelties and more casualties.

Mexico has been a violent society in many senses since the Spanish conquest began in 1519. Both violence and injustice had, however, been much reduced there since the Revolution of 1910–1917. Inevitably, however, much remains. So it was the old question of whether the bottle was half filled or half empty. The Mexican government often has thought it necessary to use forceful methods to preserve what it considers the "true revolution." Underpaid security forces committed even more illegal violent acts than those in the United States. A poor and often desperate Mexican proletariat struck out against persons and property both in frustration and anger and in hope of profit, sometimes promised by opposition political leaders.

Mexican students often have engaged in political action, but sometimes it is difficult to disentangle political motivation from high spirits and pedagogical complaints—for example, against examinations. The great student demonstrations of 1968, and the accompanying violence, excited some North Americans—including the press—unduly. One of the authors observed during that time that the numbers of people involved, surging about the streets and sidewalks, made the temptation to overreact nearly irresistible. The wild rumors that whistled about the huge Mexican capital blew up the blaze of conjecture. The approaching Olympic Games in Mexico City gave international prominence to the student "demands" and the government responses. And the deaths at Tlaltelolco on the night of October 2 gave leftists throughout the world and all dramatic reporters a fine occasion for rhetorical overkill.

It is a truism that people have a big appetite for trivia and that it can interfere with an understanding of the issues. Sometimes opinions based on trivia and ignorance led to near hysteria about Mexico when it was not justified. Notable examples occurred during the Revolution of 1910–1917. Another occurred late in Echeverría's administration in the mid-1970s, when his Third World stances, anti-American attitudes, and mildly anticapitalist remarks irritated Americans. His handling of the Mexican economy drove it into a tailspin that worried American investors and government officials.

Rumors circulated in Mexico, and were repeated in the American press, that Echeverría meant to head a coup to keep himself in office or to maintain a big influence in the following administration. Both rumors were contrary to recent Mexican tradition; probably would not be supported by the PRI, the army, organized business, or anybody else of consequence; and certainly would be resisted by the party's presidential nominee and his allies. These factors were poorly reported by the American news media, which were busy reporting the currency devaluation of August 1976 and the subsequent weakness of the peso, which set thousands of Mexicans to making wild statements to foreign reporters.

The American press seized on a few instances of violence in those months to suggest there was impending "chaos," a word that probably should be banned from all books but the Bible. The press also spoke of "hysteria" in Mexico in a sloppy and unnecessarily alarming way. One of the authors, speaking by long-distance telephone with his Mexican in-laws, detected no hysteria. But inflated language became even more common when on November 19, 1976, eleven days before the end of his term, Echeverría expropriated some rich farmland from private Mexican holders, saying they violated constitutional restrictions on the size of holdings. The lands were ordered distributed to landless peasants, who were waiting on cue on the borders of the seized lands. The rumor at once was that Echeverría meant to encourage squatters (Mexicans called them "parachutists") to take much more private land. A hullabaloo arose among partisans of private enterprise in Mexico and the United States. The fears pumped up by excitable Mexicans and Americans, and exacerbated by a sensational press, proved to be founded on merely sound and fury.

Fortunately, the shah of Iran had not yet been ousted, so that did not further induce panic and saved discriminating readers from much discussion of "trends."

Mexican Immigration as a Political Issue

Fear of illegal aliens has been growing recently in the United States, and a few people point out that the money spent on policing the Mexican border and catching illegal aliens might be better spent improving the Mexican economy. But the United States is far from panicking on the question of aliens, although a few individuals make dramatic statements, such as the senator who a few years ago spoke of the "hemorrhage" of the Mexican border. Since most Americans are little concerned, it is not surprising that there is no effective government plan to stop the entry of aliens or to put the American unemployed into the jobs the aliens fill. Of course, no one knows how to get the jobless to take such work. U.S. Secretary of Labor Ray Marshall in August 1977 was ordered by a federal judge in Virginia to approve importation of some five thousand foreign workers to pick apples in nine American states. The secretary called it a "damaging precedent" and refused to obey because nearly seven million Americans were jobless. But it turned out—as he knew it would—that he could not block all requirements for labor Americans would not perform.

Some have favored legalizing the status of illegal immigrants already in the United States, thus, they say, respecting dynamics of the free market. Others oppose that, especially if it covers all aliens who might come in the future. Some say that factories that use illegal migrants should move abroad themselves.

Few know that Western European countries have a similar problem, with more industrialized nations hosting workers from poorer European countries, as Spain, Portugal, and Italy as well as Turkey, North Africa, and South Asia. Their life in Europe is increasingly difficult because governments, under pressure, have cut or stopped the flow, and found ways to reduce slightly those already in Europe. Some are deported for violation of entry or residence terms, or other infractions of law. But the size of the foreign group has grown because they have much higher birthrates than Europeans. Thus, the foreign community in West Germany, France, Britain, Belgium, Netherlands, and Sweden grew from some 13.8 million to 14.6 million in the years 1973–1979.

The argument in Europe is much as that in the United States. Some natives want more immigrant labor, but more do not. It is said that the foreigners are dirty and ignorant. On the other hand, some Europeans feel it right to provide the foreigners with services and try to integrate them into the community. Many devices to get rid of foreigners have been tried. West Germany taxes employers who use immigrants, which helps to pay for public services for the aliens. The West German government has refused, however, to directly compensate native workers for the depressing effect on wage levels of the alien labor. France paid $2,000 to each foreign worker who agreed to go home. But, of course, some of the home countries did not want the immigrants back. Switzerland was the most ruthless in paring the size of the foreign group through deportations.

Europe also is finding that new restrictions on immigration in the better developed countries are difficult to enforce. Employers and consumers often connive at illegal entry. There may be well over one million "black market workers" in Central and Western Europe today. The oil-wealthy Middle East also is experiencing a great wave of worker immigration.

If a greatly increased American fear of immigration ever arose, it could lead to strong measures on the border and to blunt talk about Mexican population growth. Even in 1979 one heard remarks that the Mexicans should "zip it up or keep it home." Americans need to face the unpalatable fact that the immigration problem is not solvable without U.S.

investment in the Mexican economy—unless America thinks it can afford a wall.

Major Economic Issues

We have described the international requirements of the Mexican and American economies. Mexico has two great aims. The first is more economic choice and control. No sophisticated Mexican believes in economic "independence," although the notion does circulate south of the border. More control, it is thought, will help forward the second aim: to greatly enlarge and diversify the economy, improve productivity, enrich the Mexican people socially and economically, and give the nation a greater place in the world. These goals are behind all the debates we have mentioned, including those involving transnational corporations, the cost of imported science and technology, remittances of profits abroad from Mexico by foreign manufacturing affiliates, foreign investment, expansion of the tourist industry, and foisting off on the United States many of the Mexican poor.

Mexico especially wants to export more, and complains of restrictions placed on Mexican entry into the American market; that is, it wants free access to the United States for Mexican goods that can compete there, and to keep out of Mexico most United States goods that can compete south of the border. All this is highly rational, and counterbalancing. Great quantities of contraband manufactured goods from many countries are sold in Mexico, sometimes quite openly. There is no question that Mexico would prefer increased trade rather than "handouts," which it has deprecated and even refused. But some of the foreign trade favors that its requests are merely handouts of another sort.

The United States wants to continue imports of raw materials and agricultural commodities from Mexico, to ship manufactured products to Mexico, and to have an opportunity for private investment there. Washington needs to consider American producers—agricultural and industrial—who can be hurt by low-priced Mexican goods, the result of cheap wages there. And Washington has to resist Mexican criticism of restriction on this type of goods when Mexicans at the same time will not let the United States compete with some of Mexico's high-priced manufactures.

Both foreign ministries know that great economic change is unlikely to come about by diplomatic agreement, but they are reluctant to say so publicly. Echeverría told the U.N. that industrialized nations should share the wealth by buying more and higher-priced manufactures from developing countries. That probably will occur only slowly. Realistic Mexicans do not expect American aid without a quid pro quo, and are little moved by sloganeering and promises that amount to little.

We believe that there is room for expansion of Mexican tourism, that agricultural imports from Mexico to the United States could possibly be increased with proper safeguards; that yet other of Mexico's primary commodities in addition to oil might conceivably manage to improve in price relative to imported manufactured goods—possibly with a world cartel in coffee; and that almost certainly the United States would continue to be interested in importing Mexican oil and natural gas, even refined petroleum products. So there is room for some maneuvering, especially in the case of petroleum. The United States clearly considers Mexico's greatest lever to be oil, and probably Mexico is of like mind.

Certainly, without the fear of inundation by Mexican aliens Americans are unlikely to be attracted by the argument that investment in development of a neighbor eventually will pay off economically. "Eventually" is not something that most of us care to think about.

The *Washington Post* in April 1979 claimed that a majority in the United States finally was beginning to understand "the true nation-wide American stake in Mexico," because "no country is more important to the United States in terms of across-the-board, across-the-border impact on people's lives." It also claimed that in the government there was a consensus "that Mexico cannot be treated like just another Latin or middle-ranking country: It's too big, too close, too important. In some matters, such as immigration, a special relationship must be formed."

Maybe so, but most Americans still feel no urgency about Mexico. Of course, political issues oscillate in public regard, so things could change. Meanwhile, Mexico need not complain about neglect until a crisis arises; Mexico acted the same toward Guatemala. Some crises might be expected to be inflammatory. Possibly when the Mexican population reaches 100 million? 200 million? 300 million? If Mexico accepted nuclear weapons from the Soviet Union or Communist China? A communist regime in Mexico, even without bombs? Mexican insistence on selling its oil to other countries rather than the United States?

Prediction is so chancy (the authors have tried a bit in government and academic circles) that in the next chapter we provide three "scenarios" of possible development in the years ahead. A "scenario" is what government and private think tanks call a prediction in order to try to reduce criticism when it turns out to be mistaken. At least one of the scenarios presented here suggests the truth of the folk-saying with which this book began: "A well-fed neighbor sleeps, and so may you."

TEN

Three Scenarios of the Future

A Sad Scenario

Scene: TV studio. In front of cameras, four men sit: interview moderator, a Swiss; the U.N. delegate of the Republic of Québec; the U.N. delegate of the United States of Mexico; the U.N. delegate of the United States of America.

Moderator: Round table speeches are a bore, and we have agreed to have none. One minute is the limit. I will ask the first question, then others as I think useful. Otherwise, we will move clockwise—first, the delegate from Québec, then the delegate from Mexico, then the delegate from the United States. My question is: Will Mexico's charges against the United States of violations of human rights reach the United Nations General Assembly?

Québec: Certainly. Enough countries—including my own—are for it.

Mexico: The United States of North America does not even deny the charges but merely says its actions are what it calls justified.

U.S.A.: No, sir. The United States does deny that everything

209

Mexico calls violations of rights are that. Requiring English for schools and for business is not a violation of human rights, merely good sense. Mexico is just as determined that Mexicans speak Spanish.

Mexico: Three million Mexicans speak Indian languages.

U.S.A.: So do all American Indians who wish to.

Mexico: What about violent deportation of innocent Mexicans from the United States?

U.S.A.: What about answering my rebuttal on language?

Moderator: Please, can everyone wait his turn?

Québec: We in Canada rather agree with the United States on the language issue. One state, one language. Our territory suffered when we were ruled by Ottawa.

Mexico: In those years you had much more territory, did you not?

Québec: As the world knows, the brutal Anglos took 70 percent of our territory before giving us independence. And still refuse to answer to the United Nations vote that this was illegal! So we sympathize with Mexico's interest in its lost territories from Texas to California.

U.S.A.: Mr. Moderator, something seems to have happened—again—to the agreed order.

Moderator: Please, gentlemen.

U.S.A.: Communist and Third World attacks on the United States ignore our right to control entry of immigrants. All nations do so, including Mexico. The United States has been a haven for millions of poor, and those who flee a military dictatorship, like that of Mexico today. Mexico scarcely has given refuge to a handful of people in all its history.

Mexico: Will the United States delegate repudiate the assertion often heard in the U.N. today, that the United States is a fascist state?

U.S.A.: Yes. How do you feel about the charge, often heard, that the Mexican dictatorship is a tool of world communism?

Mexico: No one ever put up such a wall as the United States has erected between our countries. It is brutal and insulting.

U.S.A.: The communists built quite a wall in Germany. The Chinese put up a fair-sized one. The Romans built a number. Many European cities had walls at one time. The English used the Channel like a wall, refusing to tunnel under it. France fought for centuries for defensible boundaries—another type of wall. Mexico chooses to consider our defensive wall insulting. It was not so intended. Will the Mexican delegate explain how the wall is brutal?

Mexico: It ignores human problems—of Mexicans invited to the United States, then treated brutally.

U.S.A.: Since Mexico refused to prevent Mexicans from leaving illegally, we did so ourselves. That was our undoubted right.

Mexico: You invited them in.

U.S.A.: We cancelled the invitation.

Mexico: You had no right to take such drastic action with brutal haste and without proper discussion.

U.S.A.: We tried years of discussion. If we're speaking of rights, you had no right to a population growth of over 3 percent a year, foisting those you could not support onto us. You have 100 million now, and we hear of your plans to push them into Central America and the Caribbean. What will you do when you have 200 million?

Moderator: The population question is so delicate. . . .

U.S.A.: The Mexican delegate should reply.

Mexico: I agree with the moderator that the United States attitude makes discussion of the matter impossible.

U.S.A.: Pooh. You don't know what to say.

Québec: Mr. Moderator, can't this be kept on a civilized plane?

U.S.A.: Well, I'll change the subject. Mexico supports on its soil a group that calls itself the "Chicano Government in Exile." How would Québec like it if we fostered a "Québec Government in Exile"?

Québec: I consider the question irrelevant.

U.S.A.: The entire U.N. consideration of the Mexican charges is irrelevant.

Moderator: Because the United States has the veto power in the Security Council?

U.S.A.: Not only for that reason.

Moderator: Could we turn to the charges concerning American deportation of aliens?

Québec: Over four million men, women, and children simply dumped over the border in four or five months. It was inhuman!

Mexico: A crime!

U.S.A.: They were fed and housed.

Mexico: And simply thrown into a country unready to receive them.

U.S.A.: Unready and unwilling in every sense. You should have been ready. Besides, we offered $100 million a month in foodstuffs, for three years.

Mexico: Admitting your responsibility.

U.S.A.: To help Mexico perform its duty to its own citizens.

Moderator: It certainly seems to much of the world that between the colossal wall—surely unprecedented, despite what the American delegate says—the massive deportations, and the harrying of children for speaking Spanish, that Americans are paranoid about homogenizing their population.

U.S.A.: Spoken like a Swiss neutral and impartial moderator.

Moderator: I am proud of Swiss neutrality, and of our pluralistic culture—including, you may know, four official languages.

U.S.A.: Yes, in four languages the Swiss reject any responsibility that matters in international affairs. They never help anyone at any risk to themselves. Nor has their pluralistic society attracted many imitators. Abraham

Lincoln thought division dangerous. Many throughout the world today think the same.

Mexico: It has become impossible for Mexicans and North Americans to speak together!

U.S.A.: So it seems. I regret that.

Mexico: I also. And we have not touched many important issues—such as your country's refusal to trade with Mexico.

U.S.A.: Or yours to sell us petroleum, while you sell it to neutrals and our enemies.

Mexico: Or your refusal to let tourists visit us.

U.S.A.: Who would want to, when Mexicans insult them?

Mexico: With reason.

U.S.A.: No doubt that was why you seized all U.S.-owned property in Mexico.

Moderator: Perhaps it is time for new efforts at compromise.

U.S.A.: Things change. It is difficult to go back.

Mexico: Very difficult.

The two sheriff's deputies in uniform stood in the night by their patrol car, staring at the searchlights playing on the wall.

"Looks spooky, don't it, Bill?"

"Yeah. I was a kid, we used to swim in the river—about here, I think." They peered at the twenty-foot high concrete wall. There were no openings. A lighted guard tower to the west was only a few hundred yards away. The one to the east was much farther, where the lights of the suburbs of El Paso began. "Hard to tell exactly."

"Yeah. Wouldn't know Mexico was there at all—except when they shoot over it."

"Hear about the mortar last night?"

"Where?"

"California. Lobbed twenty or thirty shells from Tijuana into San Diego."

"Not the Mex government?"

"No. Private."

"What'd we shoot back?"

"Paper says about a hundred mortar rounds. M'wife says the Mexican radio says thousands, includin' nuclear charges."

"Your wife, she understands the Mex pretty good?"

"Spoke it at home. Both parents Mex. Our kids sure as hell only speak English."

They both nodded. Bill asked, "See the TV program last night about the U.N.?"

"Yeah. Our guy did real good."

"Fuckin' U.N. Two-bit countries tryin' to get a handout."

"Your wife must feel bad."

"Yeah. We used to go down all the time in our camper, huntin' and fishin', 'n sometimes to the beach in winter. Real cheap, you did it that way."

"Get along OK with the Mex down there?"

"Oh, sure." He seemed surprised. "No problem."

"Course, your wife's got the lingo."

"Yeah, that helped." He rubbed thoughtfully at his jaw. "But we all just seemed to get along fine."

"Maybe you'll get back some day."

"Hope so." He hesitated, then said, "Tell you the truth, this damned wall gives me the willies."

"Yeah. Well, let's go'n report in."

The Soviet colonel was bored. "I can merely repeat that it is a losing game for Mexico, Colonel Gámiz. Either you stop private citizens from shooting into the United States, or you suffer retaliation."

The Mexican colonel said savagely, "They are brutal about it. Ten, a hundred, for one."

The Soviet colonel said gravely, "Possibly they learned it from their Jews."

The Mexican looked puzzled. "How is that?"

"In Israel, they retaliated like that against the Palestine Liberation Organization."

The Mexican nodded, impatient with ancient history. "Well, sir, what am I to say to the general about our request?"

The Soviet colonel said formally, "That the Soviet Union regrets that it cannot increase weapons for the defensive area of the Mexico-United States border. That it advises Mexico, again, to evacuate as many civilians as it can from the area— say, within ten kilometers of the border. That Soviet policy must remain dedicated to (a) the defense of the heartland of Mexico and (b) confronting the United States with a retaliatory nuclear threat from artillery, aircraft, and rockets in Mexico."

The Mexican colonel said gloomily, "I'll probably be back tomorrow."

The Soviet officer said politely, "Always a pleasure, Colonel Gámiz." Then he straightened slightly. "Possibly your general will become accustomed."

Colonel Gámiz loooked startled. "No! No Mexican likes to take orders from outsiders."

The president of the United States said, "I'll have to oppose it, Fred."

The national leader of the AFL-CIO said flatly, "Low wages in the border area were bad for labor for a hundred years. We're going to have to raise them, now that Mexican labor's dried up."

"It'll push up food prices, especially if you go as fast as you're proposing."

"It'll raise wages and they'll be able to afford more."

The president shrugged. "No use going over it all again. I'm going to ask Congress to let us enforce the wage freeze more strictly." He looked thoughtfully at the labor leader. "Did you ever think that maybe the immigrant labor was valuable to us?"

The labor leader said firmly, "No, Mr. President. It threatened to suck the heart right out of organized labor."

"You don't miss those tomatoes and strawberries from Mexico in winter?"

The labor man smiled wryly. "Mine come from racist South Africa. I'll bet you eat them, too."

The president asked, "What about the busboys and maids?"

The labor leader said, with emphasis, "The wives of labor leaders aren't allowed to have maids, and if they want to eat out they can pay what decent restaurant wages make necessary or eat in cafeterias. There's just nothing about cheap alien workers you can sell to the American labor movement."

A bit later in the day the president was trying to find a chink in a different armor. "But Harry, you know what happened when we tried it without gas rationing."

Senator Gardener said stubbornly, "It's not working with rationing. The ration's too small."

"For some of your leading constitutents, I take it?"

"Some folks need more gas than others."

The president said, with obvious patience, "And the rationing system provides for that."

"Not well enough," the senator argued. "Seems to me we should go back to letting the market distribute the gas."

The president said sharply, "You know what that led to. Lots of people couldn't afford five dollars a gallon for gas."

The senator retorted, "They've got to give up more of their cars."

"Does that include senators?"

The senator ignored that. "The new railroads and streetcars and subways and bus lines can handle it."

"Thanks, Harry," the president said sarcastically. "You don't care how much political trouble you plan for me. And I have a feeling it's not just because we're in different parties."

The senator smiled. "Now, Mr. President, you've handled worse. You've got those dandy emergency powers we voted you. Hell, the press can hardly print anything you don't like. And that new national police: 300,000 men dolled up in fancy uniforms and carrying machine pistols."

The president asked curiously, "You don't worry, Harry, what all this coercive power is doing to us?"

The senator said sharply, "What choice do we have—with Soviet rockets in Mexico, and Central America and the Caribbean about to be divided between Mexico and Cuba and the Soviet Union." He paused, then continued angrily, "I suppose you haven't decided to put a stop to that."

The president said coldly, "The Senate Foreign Relations Committee is consulted at the appropriate times." And, he thought to himself, "Thank God, Harry Gardener is not on that."

The same night the National Security Council met for three hours. Afterward, the secretary of state stayed on with the president of the United States.

"So," the president said wearily, "if we invade Mexico, or stop its take-over of Central America, the Soviet Union invades Turkey and Greece and Iran, and maybe more. Then what?"

The secretary said, "Mexico expands till it meets Brazilian expansion."

The president asked gloomily, "So we have no choice but to pour all we can into Brazilian development—and expansion—so it won't fall into the Soviet sphere, too?"

The secretary nodded, "I thought you agreed."

"Oh, I agree, but it would have been cheaper and safer to help develop Mexico a few years ago."

"There was little support for it, sir, as you remember," the secretary pointed out. "Possibly," he continued impassively, "we could try again, Mr. President."

"That won't work," the president said impatiently. "You know they don't trust me." He looked at the expressionless face of his secretary of state. "Oh, I see what you mean, John. I suppose I could resign. Do you think I should, John?"

"It would be a remarkable act, sir."

The president nodded gravely, "All of that, John, all of that."

The president of Mexico dropped the message form on his desk and said to his young private secretary, "Tegucigalpa is secured. All the Central American republics in our hands before noon."

"And Washington merely blustered!" The young secretary was exultant.

The president observed moodily, "When I was your age, Pepe, we sneered at military men and condemned imperialism."

The secretary protested, "Washington had us under its thumb."

"It's certainly a different thumb now," the president agreed.

"We've increased our national territory 20 percent in one day," the secretary gloated. "We have room for the Mexican people."

The president said sourly, "Yes, we can postpone the population question again." He looked curiously at the young man. "You know, Pepe, we now have a border with Colombia, and its population grows faster than ours. Are we going to let poor Colombians into the greater Mexico?"

"I've thought about that, Mr. President."

"I thought you probably had, Pepe. And what do you recommend?"

"Naturally, we must control it."

"Naturally."

"But there are some tasks for which we have difficulty recruiting adequate hands."

The president nodded solemnly. "Your wife lose another maid who decided factory work was more dignified?"

The secretary smiled. "Something like that, Mr. President. I should remind you that the Chief of the Combined Staffs will be here in a moment. He wants to discuss the political role of the military in the new territories."

The president said, "I am ready for the battle."

"I beg pardon, sir?"

"Merely an attempted witticism, Pepe. You must learn to ignore them. It is an affectation of the aged."

The secretary was polite. "Yes, Mr. President."

"Relax, Pepe," the president said kindly. "I gather that you approve of General Bueno?"

"I find him impressive, Mr. President. When I studied at the Diplomatic Institute, he addressed my class."

The president said dryly, "On the 'Greater Mexican Sphere of Activity in Alliance with the Soviet Union,' no doubt."

"No, sir," the secretary said seriously. "His subject was 'A Giant Should Be Respected.' "

The president said musingly, "It wasn't what I was brought up to, but I can live with that."

A Rosy Scenario

The chairman of the Central Executive Committee of the Communist party of Mexico was sixty-nine years old and looked it. "You have the list, Alicia?"

"Yes," said the secretary. She passed him a paper as she sat down by his desk.

The chairman regarded the list without enthusiasm. "Not too inspiring."

Alicia was a phlegmatic and formless forty. "No," she agreed unhelpfully.

"Nevertheless," the chairman said doggedly, "we must have a program to recommend by three this afternoon."

The woman waited, pencil in slack fingers.

"We can," the chairman said without conviction, "attack the new Mexico-United States joint citizenship as destructive of Mexicanidad."

When the secretary did not react, the chairman said sharply, "What's your reaction to that, Alicia?"

"People like dual citizenship," she said stolidly.

"I know that," the chairman said testily. "We're talking about tactics."

Alicia shrugged. "I can only think of one, Pedro."

The chairman looked at her suspiciously. "And?"

"A long vacation."

"That is not amusing."

"My God!" the woman said. "It wasn't meant to be. What I meant to say was—a period of inaction to redevelop planning in the light of altered circumstances."

The chairman looked aggrieved. "We've been in the party together a long time, Alicia. You needn't be sarcastic."

The secretary threw her dictation book on the desk and brought out a cigarette. "It wasn't just sarcasm. I'm nervous. Nobody seems to make any mistakes but us."

"Moscow, too," the chairman said comfortingly.

"I was including them with us," the secretary said.

The chairman looked at the list again. "Well, we can start another campaign against selling all our surplus petroleum and natural gas to the United States at twenty percent above world prices—if we can find a new twist."

"Don't look at me," Alicia disclaimed. "It's hopeless. People think we're screwing the gringos. That seems to have corrupted everyone."

The chairman read from the list. "Possibly 20 million Mexicans now work in the United States. Is that the new official figure?"

The secretary blew smoke out with a laugh. "I made it up."

"Your mother, with the jokes!" exploded the chairman. "I like to know what I'm talking about."

Alicia said soothingly, "The last government figure was over 18 million. No doubt it's gone up."

"I suppose so," the chairman said apathetically. "We can claim again that the bilingual schools in the United States are a fake."

"We can," Alicia agreed, "but no one would believe it. Really, Pedro, all I can think of is either population control or free trade. At least they are so complex that there's some room for maneuvering."

The chairman threw the list on his desk and lit a cigar. "My sister's head of the State of Michoacán Birth Control League."

"That the one married to a road builder?"

"Yes. They could afford a hundred children."

Alicia said firmly, "It's gone out of fashion. Even in Russia."

"That," said the chairman, "leaves us with free trade. 'Mexico increasingly subservient to the Money-Masters of Wall Street?' "

Alicia looked doubtful. "Not very punchy." She said the word in English.

"Shit! Do you have to use those English terms?"

The secretary said testily, "Even Lenin used foreign terms when he wanted to be punchy."

The chairman said despondently, "We could say that the new alliance with the United States is threatening the beauty of the Spanish language."

"Oh, boy," Alicia said in English, "Que idea comunista."

And they lived happily ever after.

A Moderate Scenario

The Mexican diplomat raised his glass. "Salud! Not a bad session, Ray."

The State Department man looked moodily around the crowded bar. "Not for you, Luis. Christ! Twenty percent over world prices for your oil."

The Mexican smiled. "What you and I learned at Harvard Business School, Ray. The parts of a rational solution may seem irrational."

"We gave up our transportation advantage."

"You don't have any unless we give it to you."

"Damn it, Luis, it's five times as far to Indonesia as to Mexico. That's a natural advantage."

The Mexican smiled again, "Harvard Business taught us that nature has no vote."

The American said, "I didn't realize you were taking our student days so much to heart. I suppose Harvard Business told you how we can solve the political problem of such an agreement."

"Oh," Luis protested, "I would not dream of interfering in your political process. I am sure you can just say that the Mexicans held you up."

"That'll make us look great."

"You'll get sympathy."

The American said sarcastically, "Thanks. Pity, more likely, and pity in politics buys nothing."

The Mexican said sharply, "The oil won't buy us too much, either, Ray. You'll raise the prices of computers and machinery."

The American nodded, smiling. "You've cheered me up. Here's to Harvard Business School."

"Come on, Don. You know that an international agreement requires compromises."

Senator Donald Parker said, "You gave Arizona's water to Mexico, Mr. President, and folks at home are mad."

The president asked, "You have enough water right now?"

The senator looked at him suspiciously. "You know we don't. California takes too much."

The president said impatiently, "The Colorado River doesn't have enough for all the users. You know that, Don."

"Everybody knows that, Mr. President."

The president said earnestly, "So you give up some Colorado water, and—"

"Sure," the senator from Arizona exclaimed. "The treaty gives Mexico five times as much as it gets now. They get more from the Colorado River than all the American users put together. And the river runs two thousand miles in the United States and a lousy hundred in Mexico."

"When?"

"When what?" the senator asked.

"When," the president asked, "does Mexico get all that Colorado water?"

The senator looked disgusted. "Oh, I read the treaty, Mr.

President. You're talking about the fine print. Voters don't care about the fine print."

"I'll bet you do, though, Don," the president said.

The senator flapped a hand, settled back in his chair, and got out a cigar. His face became a shade less red. "Sure, I read the fine print in personal contracts—and everything else. But voters are jumpy."

The president said, "I'm going to explain it on TV."

"That may help," the senator conceded.

"They don't lose any Colorado River water till the Alaska pipe is in, and that's out of federal money."

"Voters aren't much interested in the future, Mr. President."

"I know," the president agreed. "I spend a lot of time thinking about voters, too, Don."

The senator chuckled. "The Colorado's real close. It seems more real than Alaska."

The president nodded. "I'll tell them they won't lose a gallon of that lousy salty river till the Alaska stuff is flowing in, clear and sparkling."

The senator asked, "What do you really suppose the Alaska water project's going to cost us, Mr. President?"

The president said coolly, "I'm not interested."

The senator asked in surprise, "How's that? Won't you have to be? It'll ruin the budget."

"Not mine," the president said complacently.

The senator looked startled. "You've got five more years— if you're reelected."

"I expect to be reelected, Don."

"You mean, you're not going to build the Alaska line?"

The president looked almost benign. "I mean that I expect that the Congress will insist on prolonged feasibility studies."

The senator seemed to find that a pleasing idea. "I'm sure we will. Let 'em wait a piece."

"I am sure," the president said gravely, "that the Mexicans are not unprepared for that."

The girl on the beach towel accepted a glass from the young man. "Thanks, Ricky. How was Washington?"

"Cold," he said, taking off the jacket of his conservative dark suit. "I'll go up and change. Just wanted to be sure you were here, Meg."

"Did you make brilliant speeches, Ricky?"

"Hagghh!" The young man was disgusted. "At my level in the Mexican Foreign Ministry, your longest speech is, 'Si, señor.' Why did your father bring you here?"

The girl shrugged. "Dad says Acapulco's ugly and dirty. So Ixtapa's where we are."

"I still love you," the young man said.

The girl did not appear too grateful. "So it's lasted another two weeks."

"And it will last another two years." He was irritated.

"Is that what we'll put in the marriage contract?" she asked. "Good for two years?"

The young man threw his coat onto the girl's beach towel, and sank to his knees in the sand beside her. "Your sister's problems have nothing to do with us, Meg. Some international marriages work."

"Dad calls them cross-cultural marriages."

"What's the difference?" the young man said impatiently.

The girl said with mock gravity, "Dad says that if you don't know the difference, you don't know the problem."

The Mexican said, smiling with conscious charm, "I know the difference. I know the problem." He took her hand. "Come on, Meg, let's get married and have some Mexican-American children. The boys can go into your father's business, which will boom under the new treaty we just cleverly arranged."

"Were you really clever?" she asked derisively. "Dad says treaties seldom are even half-intelligent. What'd you do about drugs, tell me that."

The Mexican sat in the sand, pulled off his shirt and shoes.

"OK, you'll see how bright your future husband is. We agreed that drugs are an internal United States problem, and that population growth is a Mexican problem."

She protested, "You didn't! That's no solution at all."

"We dressed it up a little," he added. "Mexico will do its utmost to ameliorate the conditions that lead to illegal immigration to the United States, while the United States will make equally vigorous efforts to ameliorate the conditions that induce drug smuggling from Mexican territory."

She was indignant. "But it doesn't change anything."

"Not immediately," he agreed. "But, little innocent, it was a master stroke."

"Little innocent, yourself. It's a nothing."

He grinned at her and said, "It made it easier to change a lot of other things."

"Such as?"

"Things that let your father's Superior Electronics build fifty-five factories in Mexico."

She smiled. "He'll love that."

"I know he will. That's why I did it. So that when I come to dinner he'll feel more kindly toward cross-cultural marriages."

Meg's father was on the long-distance telephone in his suite in the Ixtapa Hilton.

"OK, Bill. That's clear. In effect, the United States agreed to drop a lot of labor-intensive manufacturing, and let Mexico take over and sell us the stuff. And we concentrate on capital-intensive production. That's us. . . . Sure, sure, the pants and shoe manufacturers will howl. You get to work howling them down."

The president of the American Farm Federation said to his chief lobbyist, "Tom, we've got to stop ratification of the Mexican treaty."

"It'll be tough."

"We'll get a lot of sympathy. It lets cheap Mexican farmers destroy the small farmer in this country."

The lobbyist said, "Lots of agribusiness will be for the treaty. They'll sell plenty of wheat and corn to Mexico."

The president said sharply, "The American Farm Federation is made up of small and medium-size farmers."

"I know, I know. I'm just saying it will be tough. Lots of people'll be glad to get Mexican tomatoes and strawberries and vegetables."

"For Christ's sake, Tom! Don't tell me the problem. Tell me the solution."

"I'm happy," said the U.S. secretary of state, "that you could agree to this private meeting after the signing of the treaty."

The Mexican minister of foreign relations nodded. "It seems to me that we have some things to discuss."

The secretary of state smiled. "Such as how long will it take to make the new treaty work well?"

The Mexican made an expressive gesture. "We know the answer to that. A long time." He asked casually, "How soon do you think your Alaska water flow will release the Colorado River water to Mexico?"

"Sooner, I imagine, sir, than your population growth will be as low as two percent a year."

"The long view," observed the Mexican, "is so apt to be discouraging." He smiled slightly. "Also the short view."

The secretary of state nodded. "A friend of mine used to say that foreign relations is not gleeful. What I wanted to briefly explore with you, sir, is the possibility that in the gleeful future, Mexico, the United States, and Canada might want to consider some sort of economic union."

The Mexican looked interested. "It is the trend of the times, as the young men in my ministry insist. They like to show me computer printouts."

"You and I will be gone," the secretary of state observed, "before such a union can be discussed seriously."

The Mexican said heavily, "I know. Mexico will have to change its society in order to be a full partner with the United States and Canada."

The secretary of state said kindly, "It will be a large task, certainly. My young men's computer printouts say that by then Mexico's population will be about 180 million, ours maybe 250 million, and Canada's 40 million, not counting Québec of course."

The Mexican agreed. "It will be difficult enough without the distraction of mini-states." He added musingly, "A community market of nearly 500 million inhabitants." His face grew guardedly complacent, and the American secretary of state wondered if he was selling tomatoes and Datsuns "Hecho en Mexico" to Kentucky and Saskatchewan.

Afterword

Some version of one—or all—of the three scenarios no doubt will come to pass. That is ensured by the fact that the principal problems will remain to plague the neighbors. We hope that the worst of reality will be only moderately bad or sad and that considerable parts of the best will be at least moderately pleasant. *"Ojalá,"* as the Mexicans say—"God willing."

It is nice to dream of a really triumphant rapprochement, but for that we need to depend on the old prayer

> Rejoice us, O Lord,
> With thought of our need,
> Rather than our merit.

Additional Reading

GENERAL

Karl Schmitt, *Mexico and the United States, 1821-1973* (New York: John Wiley, 1974). Covers all aspects of Mexico-United States relations. Robert Jones Shafer, *A History of Latin America* (Lexington, Mass.: D.C. Heath, 1978). Mexican history and economic development.

THE BORDERLANDS

Paul Horgan, *Great River: The Rio Grande in North American History*, 2 vols. (New York: Minerva Press, 1954). Oscar J. Martinez, *Border Boom Town: Ciudad Juarez Since 1848* (Austin: University of Texas Press, 1978).

MORE ON MEXICO

T. R. Fehrenbach, *Fire and Blood: A History of Mexico* (New York: Macmillan, 1973); Roger Hansen, *Mexican Economic Development: The Roots of Rapid Growth* (Washington; Government Printing Office, 1971), and *The Politics of Mexican Development* (Baltimore: Johns Hopkins University Press, 1971); J. Richard Powell, *The Mexican Petroleum Industry, 1938-1950* (Los Angeles and Berkeley: The University of California Press, 1956); Clark W. Reynolds, *The Mexican Economy: Twentieth Century Structure and Growth* (New Haven: Yale University Press, 1970).

MEXICAN-AMERICANS

David J. Weber, et al., *Foreigners in Their Native Land: Historical Roots of the Mexican Americans* (Albuquerque: University of New Mexico Press, 1973); Vernon Briggs, Jr., et al., *The Chicano Worker* (Austin: University of Texas Press, 1977); John H. Burma, comp., *Mexican-Americans in the United States* (Cambridge: Schenkman, 1970); Carlos E. Castañeda, *Our Catholic Heritage in Texas, 1519-1936*, 7 vols. (Austin: University of Texas Press, 1936-1958); Mark Day *Forty Acres: Cesar Chávez and the Farm Workers* (New York: Praeger, 1971); E. B. Fincher, *Spanish-Americans as a Political Factor in New Mexico, 1912-1950* (New York: Arno, 1974); David Gómez, *Somos Chicanos: Strangers in Our Own Land* (Boston: Beacon, 1973); Nancie González, *The Spanish Americans of New Mexico* (Albuquerque: University of New Mexico Press, 1969); Leo Grebler, et al., *The Mexican-American People: The Nation's Second Largest Minority* (New York: Free Press, 1970); Norris Hundley, Jr., ed., *The Chicano* (Santa Barbara: American Bibliographical Center, 1975); Francisco J. Lewels, Jr., *The Uses of the Media by the Chicano Movement: A Study of Minority Access* (New York: Praeger, 1974); Ed Ludwig and James Santibanezm, eds., *The Chicanos. Mexican American Voices* (Baltimore: Penquin Books, 1971); Carey McWilliams, *North from Mexico; the Spanish-Speaking People of the United States* (Philadelphia, 1949; reprinted New York, Greenwood Press, 1968); Joan W. Moore and Alfredo Cuellar, *Mexican Americans*, 2d ed. (Englewood Cliffs, N.J.: Prentice Hall, 1976); Wayne Moquin and Charles Van Doren, eds., *A Documentary History of the Mexican Americans* (New York: Praeger, 1971; Bantam Books, 1972); Leonard Pitt, *The Decline of the Californios: A Social History of the Spanish-Speaking Californians, 1846-1890* University of California Press, 1966); Mark Reisler, *By the Sweat of Their Brow: Mexican Immigrant Labor in the United States, 1900-40* (Westport: Greenwood Press, 1976); George I. Sanchez, *Forgotten People: A Study of the New Mexicans* (Albuquerque: University of New Mexico Press, 1940); Edward Simmen, ed., *The Chicano: From Caricature to Self-Portrait* (New York: New American Library, 1971); Stan Steiner, *La Raza: The Mexican Americans* (New York: Harper and Row, 1970); Ellwyn Stoddard, *Mexican Americans* (New York, Random, 1973).

SOME MEXICO-UNITED STATES PROBLEMS

Richard B. Mancke, *Mexican Oil and Natural Gas: Political, Strategic, and Economic Implications* (New York: Praeger, 1979); Clarence Clendenen, *Blood on the Border. The United States Army and the Mexican Irregulars* (New York: Macmillan, 1969), Richard B. Craig, *The Bracero Program: Interest Groups and Foreign Policy* (Austin:

University of Texas Press, 1971); Ernesto Galarza, *Merchants of Labor: The Mexican Bracero Story* (San Jose: Rosicrucian Press, 1965); Manuel Gamio, *Mexican Immigration to the United States: A Study of Human Migration and Adjustment* (Chicago: University of Chicago Press, 1930); Abraham Hoffman, *Unwanted Mexican Americans in the Great Depression: Repatriation Pressures, 1929-39* (Tempe: University of Arizona Press, 1974); Norris Hundley, *Dividing the Waters: A Century of Controversy Between the United States and Mexico* (Berkeley: University of California Press, 1966); Manuel Machado, *An Industry in Crisis. Mexico-United States Cooperation in the Control of Foot-and-Mouth Disease* (Berkeley: University of California Press, 1968); Lorenzo Meyer, *Mexico and the United States in the Oil Controversy, 1917-42* (Austin: University of Texas Press, 1977); Stanley R. Ross, ed., *Views Across the Border. The United States and Mexico* (Albuquerque: University of New Mexico Press, 1979); Robert Freeman Smith, *The United States and Revolutionary Nationalism in Mexico, 1916-32* (Chicago: University of Chicago Press, 1972); Walter P. Webb, *The Texas Rangers: A Century of Frontier Defense* (Austin: University of Texas Press, 1965).

Index

235